PEARL HARBOR

PEARL HARBOR

H.P. WILLMOTT

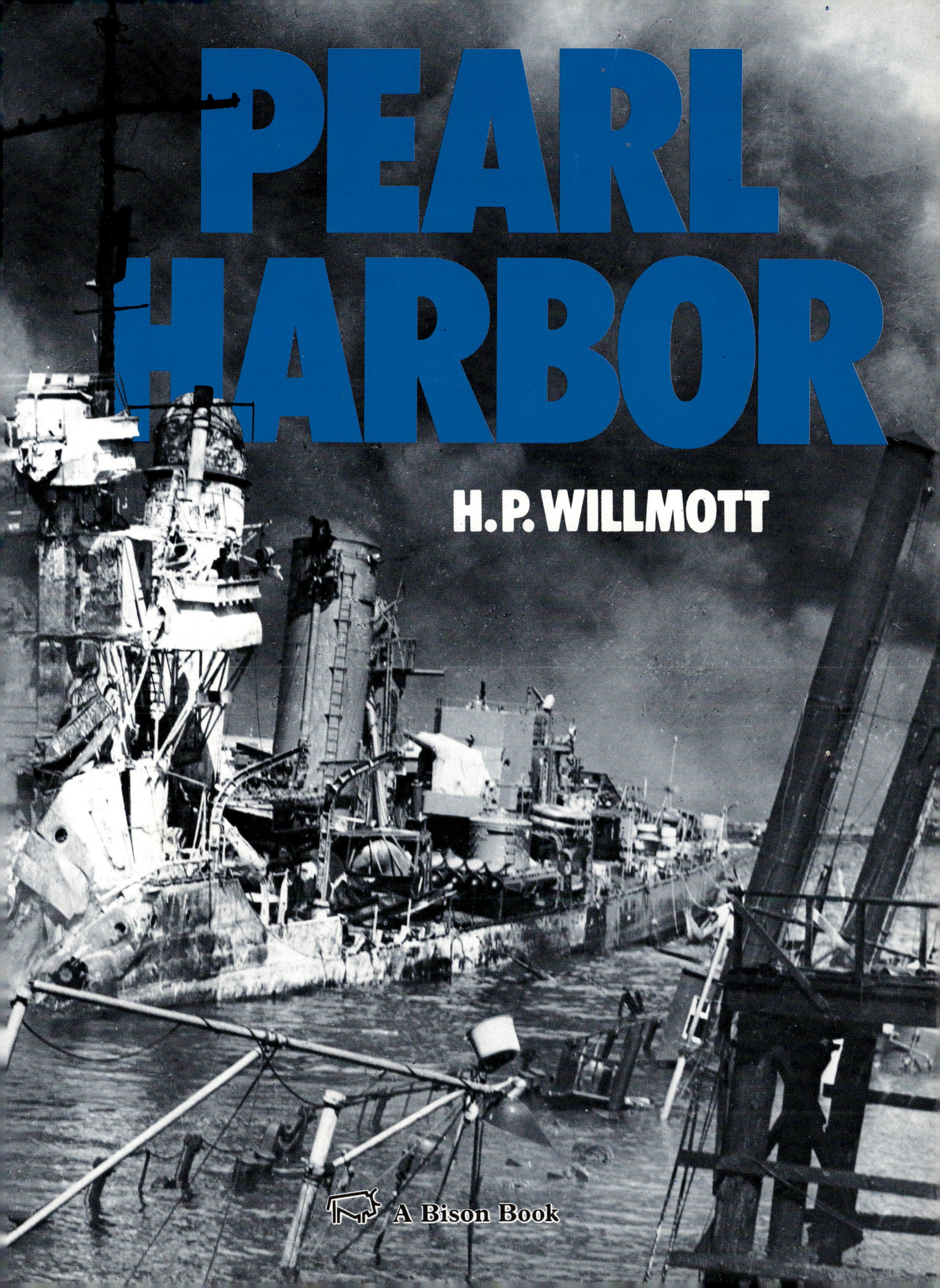

A Bison Book

First Published in the UK by
Bison Books Ltd
4 Cromwell Place
London SW7

Produced by Bison Books Ltd

ISBN 0 86124 033 2

Printed in Hong Kong

CONTENTS

Page 1: Disregarding the possibility of explosions, US sailors fight the flames on USS *West Virginia*.
Page 2–3: USS *Shaw* in floating drydock after the attack.
Page 4–5: Sailors rearming clips and belts during the attack.

1. THE QUEST FOR SUPREMACY

Mythology tells of Japan's divine origins and character. Ruled by a god-emperor, the Tenno, who was the direct descendant of the chief deity, Amaterasu, the sun-goddess, it was a land watched over by the lesser gods, and inhabited by a semi-divine chosen people. The Japanese, who saw death in the service of their Tenno as insufficient atonement for the debt they owed their homeland, regarded themselves as being charged with a divine mission. This mission, their manifest destiny, was the domination and leadership of eastern Asia.

Divinity, however, has its limits. Heavenly kingdoms may run on faith and worship, but earthly ones run on oil, and a whole host of raw materials without which ordered society cannot survive. Divine purpose, moreover, can be balked by the capriciousness of man. In the 1930s, as Japan sought to assume the leadership and control of eastern Asia by starting with the progressive and bloody conquest of China, it became increasingly obvious that not many people outside Japan shared her view of her heaven-sent mandate.

Fate dictated that Japan was forced to operate in a political and economic world order devised by and benefitting white imperialist nations – in the Far East these nations were Britain, France, the Netherlands and the USA. These states, through their colonial possessions, stood in the way of Japan's quest for domination of the Far East. Their territories contained all the raw materials Japan needed if she was to be self-sufficient and not dependent on the white nations for her means of existence. Rubber and tin from Malaya, iron ore from the Philippines, rice from Indo-China and Burma, oil, bauxite, coal, cobalt, copra, graphite, iron, lead, nickel, phosphates and potash from the Indies were the commodities Japan needed if she was to expand. The events of 15 May 1940 brought within Japan's grasp the glittering prospect of securing these territories and their resources.

On the outbreak of war in Europe in September 1939 Japan had declared her neutrality. It was in Japan's interest to wait upon events in Europe and see how they unfolded before committing herself. Being an expansionist power, she had little to gain, and possibly much to lose, by an Anglo-French victory, but this possibility was ended by the events of 15 May. When German armor ruptured the French positions overlooking the Meuse, it made a breach that the Anglo-French armies were unable to seal. Within six weeks Britain and France were hounded to decisive defeat; France to an armistice, Britain to ineffective defiance.

The humbling of France created an entirely new situation in the Far East of which Japan immediately prepared to take advantage. The French in the interwar period had placed their faith in a series of fixed defenses along their border with Germany. These defenses were known as the Maginot Line. At its first and only test it failed France because it was outflanked. The Maginot Line was much more than the shield of France alone. It had been the shield of the United States and the guarantee of American immunity from the malignancy of Nazism. It had also been the shield that had protected the British, Dutch and French possessions in the Far East which Japan coveted. Within a matter of weeks of the prostration of France, the Japanese made a series of moves to capitalize on the powerlessness of the European colonial empires.

In the van of these moves was the Imperial Navy which had long regarded Southeast Asia as the proper area of Japanese expansion because only there could Japan find the resources she needed to achieve autarky. The navy had small regard for the Imperial Army's invasion of China, which since 1931 had secured Manchuria, northern and central China and much of coastal southern China, but which showed no sign of achieving final victory over the Nationalist Government of Chiang Kai-shek. Despite the loss of its best armies and most productive areas, the Chinese government refused to come to terms with Japan. Japan therefore found herself with an open-ended commitment to a war which she could not win militarily. Japan was without the political, diplomatic and economic leverage to end the war by other means.

Top right: Japanese machine gunners man their post in northern China.
Top far right: This Chinese soldier was killed in Shanghai in 1932.
Right: Japanese infantrymen cry 'banzai' in China, summer 1937.

Up until May 1940 the army restrained the navy's desire for movement toward Southeast Asia. It had no wish to add further complications to an unfinished war and the sensitive uncertainties of Japanese–Soviet relations. With the humbling of France the army saw the chance to isolate China from outside support, either by securing Southeast Asia or by forcing Britain, the Netherlands and Vichy France into such concessions that the same result would be achieved by peaceful means. Thus at the fateful army–navy liaison meetings in June and July 1940 the army endorsed the navy's demands for a move on the south. The two services joined together to force the resignation of the cautious government of Admiral Mitsumasa Yonai when it showed signs of being alarmed by the implications of their demands. Prince Fumimaro Konoye was appointed in Yonai's place, but the services allowed him to take office only if he agreed to an alliance with Germany and Italy, a strengthening of the armed services and a more aggressive forward strategy in Southeast Asia.

The two armed services made clear to Konoye that in demanding expansion southward they recognized and accepted the possibility of a hostile American countermove designed to prevent Japan from securing resources that in future would make her invulnerable to any form of American pressure. The navy, particularly, realized that Japan's quest for self-sufficiency might provoke the type of economic blockade of Japan by the Americans that the quest itself was designed to forestall. Though in 1940 neither service anticipated that the Americans would go to war in the immediate future, both recognized that in the long term the United States was unlikely to stand aside tamely and abandon China and the European empires to their fate. American hostility to a rearming Japan was self-evident; the Japanese held no illusions on that matter. The Americans, by a variety of actions, had consistently belittled Japan as a nation and people. Both Japanese armed services were convinced that in the final analysis war was probable, and this was accepted as the only way Japan could hope to realize her ambitions and destiny.

A war with the broken powers of Europe held no terrors for Japan, but a war with the United States was not something that the Japanese considered lightly. A conflict with the United States was certain to be a hazardous undertaking because of the vast disparity of resources between the two nations. Paradoxically, however, it was this very disparity, because it threatened not to shrink but grow, that began to force Japan toward action before it became too late to act at all.

The fall of France had forced the Americans to define their security interests. As American opinion was heavily isolationist this was no easy task, but the framework had been established even before the war. The United States had recognized that the greatest danger to her security came from Germany. Before the fall of France the United States had thought in terms of fighting a two-ocean war in association with Britain and France. The defeat of France pushed the Americans into an increasingly heavy commitment to sustain a beleaguered Britain, but it also forced them to assume the role of restraining Japan – without any help from Britain and France. Yet in 1940 America was in a weak position. Years of interwar neglect of the armed services and the demands of two oceans meant that American military, naval and air power in the Pacific in 1940 were at abysmally low levels.

With the fall of France something close to real panic gripped the United States, Congress passed a series of measures designed to strengthen the American armed services. The strength of the army and navy and their air forces was to be greatly increased but the most significant measure was the Two-Ocean Naval Expansion Act. Under its terms the Americans, at a cost of $4,000,000,000, committed themselves to building seven battleships, 18 carriers, 27 cruisers, 115 destroyers and 42 submarines to add to the 130 warships already under construction and the 358 major units in commission.

The Imperial Navy appreciated that when the act's provisions were realized, the Americans would be so powerful at sea as to be unchallengeable. Japan in time would be reduced to the second or third rank, as the new ships would be more than double the size of the US Pacific Fleet. With every year that passed Japan's chances of avoiding defeat in a war with the Americans would lessen until they became nonexistent. At this time the Imperial Navy never considered itself capable of defeating the Americans, but it did believe that it was capable of fighting a successful defensive campaign in the western Pacific – among the Carolines and Marianas – that could lead to a profitable compromise peace. It believed that it could make the reduction of Japan and her conquests so costly that the Americans would accept a negotiated peace, especially if the European situation seemed likely to result in a total German victory.

The navy's interwar planning centered around the notion of a decisive naval engagement in the western Pacific. The Japanese were prepared for war with America, knowing that with every mile the drag of logistics, strain and dispersal would eat away at American strength. The orthodoxy of the day was that for every 1000 miles a fleet operated away from its base, it lost 10 percent of its effectiveness. It was believed that it was impossible for a fleet to operate more than 2000 miles away from its bases. The Imperial Navy calculated that as long as it could maintain itself at not less than 50 percent of American strength, and as long as its ships were qualitatively superior to those of the Americans, it had every chance of fighting a successful defensive campaign in the western Pacific. In 1940 the navy estimated that the balance of naval power was 10:7 against it. When this was adjusted to take into consideration the effect of the Atlantic on American dispositions, the balance in the Pacific was strongly in Japan's favor.

The Two-Ocean Act promised to undermine this favorable Japanese position. The Japanese calculated that to match new American construction their own scheduled building program for 1942 would have to be doubled, and this was impossible. The proposed 1942 program was far in excess of the current program, which in 1940 was encountering difficulties because it was too ambitious for Japan's slender resources. In 1941 the navy calculated that the Americans were building three tons for every ton in Japanese yards, and that by 1944 the balance of naval power would be a disastrous 10:3 against it. The Imperial Navy's long-term prospects were therefore bleak.

The key factor in this situation was time. The act would only produce ships from 1943 onward, and it was not due for completion until the period 1946–48. As Japan had entered the field of naval rearmament early, her 1937 and 1939 programs would allow her to stand at the peak of her strength relative to the Americans in late 1941 or early 1942. Thus certainly for a year, and for perhaps as long as two years, the Imperial Navy would be either superior or very close to American strength in the Pacific. Thereafter American dockyards would reduce the Japanese to a position of helpless inferiority and ineffectiveness as eloquently as any decisive defeat in battle could achieve.

This was the essence of Japan's strategic problem. She had to find a way of avoiding inevitable relegation to the second rank without abandoning her ambitions. In the event of her trying to secure Southeast Asia she faced a further strategic problem with regard to the Americans. Between Japan and the area of her ambitions lay the Philippines, an American colony scheduled for independence in 1944. The Philippines straddled Japanese lines of communication with Southeast Asia, and on the island group were American defense installations that could be reinforced to menace any Japanese deployment southward. Moreover, Japan's southern lines of communication were also straddled by the Hawaii–Wake–Guam–Luzon–China line, though this was not too serious a problem because in Oceania the Japanese held the stronger geographical position by virtue of their possessions in the Marianas, Carolines and Marshalls. If the Japanese moved against Southeast Asia they could not afford to leave these American positions unreduced, and they could not risk leaving the whole of their left flank, stretching across thousands of miles of ocean, bared to an intact and

Right: The US fleet lies at anchor at Cólon, which lies at the Caribbean end of the Panama Canal. This waterway provided a vital link between the Pacific and Atlantic.

Above: Japanese troops man their positions during the siege of Shanghai in the summer of 1937.
Right: Prince Konoye with members of his cabinet in 1937.

alerted US Pacific Fleet at its base in Pearl Harbor. This was the only force capable of offering effective resistance to Japan.

Japan's strategy was the responsibility of the Imperial Government and the Naval General Staff but in fact one man came to dominate the strategic planning of the Imperial Navy in the two years before the Pearl Harbor operation. That man was Admiral Isoruku Yamamoto, Commander in Chief of the Combined Fleet, the senior executive officer in the Imperial Navy. The plan to attack the US Pacific Fleet at its base in Pearl Harbor was his brain child, though he would have been the first to acknowledge the help he received in forming the plan – not least from American sources.

Yamamoto was a practical, realistic patriot. He shared Japanese ambitions in the Far East, but he knew from first-hand experience, gained as a student at Harvard and later as a naval attaché in Washington, of the awesome power and potential of American industry. He was outspoken in his opposition to a war with the Americans because he had no confidence in the ultimate outcome of such a conflict. He was trapped by the drift toward war, and he believed that war might be forced upon Japan if she was to retain her world position and self-respect. From the time of his appointment as Commander in Chief in August 1939, Yamamoto's mind turned to the problem the Americans posed to Japanese ambitions. His strategic acumen told him the obvious points: that he could not rely on American nonintervention in the event of a Japanese move on Southeast Asia; that he dare not leave an open flank across the width of the Pacific and that American construction was too great a long-term threat to be ignored. Increasingly he became convinced that if a war was inevitable then it was desirable that it be induced and not delayed. He was also increasingly convinced that the only way out of Japan's strategic difficulties was to find a way of striking a decisive blow that would crush the Americans and equalize accounts between the two nations either at the start of a war or shortly after.

This was just what the Japanese had done in 1904 against the Russians. Indeed, the Russo–Japanese conflict and the wars against China in 1894, 1931 and 1937, had certain points to offer Yamamoto as he

Below: A Japanese howitzer battery during the siege of Port Arthur in the Russo-Japanese War of 1904–05.

Bottom: The Russian defenders of Port Arthur in action against Japanese warships.

Bottom right: After the capitulation of the Russian garrison the defenders were allowed to evacuate the port, as depicted by this war artist's painting.

deliberated over the problem of the Americans. In all these conflicts the Japanese had attacked without the formality of a declaration of war. In the Russo–Japanese war the Japanese had started hostilities with a night attack on the main Russian fleet base at Port Arthur with their light forces. It was an attack from which the Russians never recovered, psychologically and materially. For the rest of the war the Russian battle squadron barely left harbor and finally succumbed to indirect fire from the Japanese army, attacking the harbor-fortress from landward.

The Russo–Japanese war, and the Sino–Japanese war of 1894, were major milestones in Japan's emergence as a major power, and the outcome of these wars, plus the manner in which she fought them, had major effects on Japan's political and strategic values and concepts. In both conflicts Japan fought and defeated nations that on paper were vastly superior to herself. From these wars Japan drew the confidence, which became dangerously unbalanced, that she need not fear superior numbers. Superior morale, it was believed, would see Japan through against the odds. Japanese martial prowess, *Nihon Seishin*, based upon an acceptance, even readiness, to die in imperial service, was the critical factor in the balancing of the odds. The planners were also aware that certain hard-headed military factors of a more orthodox and pragmatic nature were basic considerations in the triumphs on either side of the turn of the century.

Both the Sino–Japanese and Russo–Japanese wars had been primarily fought on land, but the basis of Japanese victory in both conflicts had been sea power. In these wars Japan's navy had been inferior to its enemies, but it had enjoyed local superiority because, unlike the Chinese and Russian fleets, it had been concentrated and held the advantage of superior geographical position. This local superiority, when combined with the use of surprise and offensive action, was the means by which the Imperial Navy fought for and secured command of the seas. In this process the Japanese used their battle fleet sparingly. The battle fleet was held back, ready to give battle if the need arose, but the need had to be urgent to justify its commitment. The brunt of the task of fighting for supremacy fell to Japan's light, expendable and easily replaced warships. These were entrusted with engaging and destroying enemy battle units; if that could not be achieved then Japan's light forces were charged with inflicting on the enemy disproportionately heavy losses that would either cause a faltering of enemy resolve or allow the battle fleet to join battle under conditions of maximum advantage and minimum risk to itself. The whole essence of Japanese naval policy in both wars was the use of cheap craft, capable of quick and easy replacement, to fight for and secure supremacy at the forward edge of the battle area. In both wars this basic naval blueprint served Japan well, and the master plan contained all the basic ingredients for a plan of attack on the Americans. Yamamoto was free to draw upon them if he was to persist in his notion of attacking the Americans before they became too strong to be challenged.

If the American fleet was crippled at the outset of a war then the Japanese would be free to conquer and then consolidate their gains in reasonable security. Moreover, if a surprise attack was successful American construction would not be additional to existing strength but replacement for losses. In this way the potential disparity between the American and Japanese fleets would not necessarily materialize, or if it did would not become too serious. The Americans would be forced to feed their newly commissioned ships into action in a piecemeal manner so the Japanese could hope to maintain themselves above the crucial 50 percent margin. Thereby a successful attritional campaign could be fought in the western Pacific with every confidence.

The Japanese plan of attack on Pearl Harbor has been called many things, few of which have been complimentary. It is normally portrayed as imbecilic or an act of suicide because it was certain to be self-defeating, but it was not necessarily any such thing. It was an action shaped and determined by Japanese historical experience and deeply entrenched in the mainstream of Japanese strategic and psychological values. It was the response to what was virtually an impossible strategic situation. The plan was logically conceived and carefully reasoned, and it formed part of an overall strategy which, despite its weaknesses and certain unrealities, was rational, calculated and ruthless.

2. PLANS AND PREPARATIONS

Detailed planning and preparation for the Pearl Harbor attack was extremely thorough. The problem of relating the plan's gestation, however, is that it separates into distinct parts, not all of which are in phase with one another. Firstly, there was the development and then the enunciation of the idea itself. The idea was mooted for the first time in November 1940. Secondly, there was the detailed planning stage. The initial plans were drawn up by March 1941 and, with the exception of certain very important details, were completed by May. Thirdly, predating both and continuing right up until the first week in November was the series of exercises to which the forces, particularly the aircrew, earmarked for the attack were subjected. Fourthly, from May onward there was a series of arguments within the Imperial Navy over whether or not to accept the plan. Formal endorsement of the plan was only given as late as 3 November by the Chief of the Naval General Staff, Admiral Osami Nagano. This was just three days before the final exercises before the attack and less than two weeks before the first units detailed for the attack sailed on their missions. Fifthly, there was the deteriorating international situation throughout 1941 which added urgency to the Japanese quest to solve their problem of if, when and how to go to war. Eventually on 23 November the main task force for the attack received its orders to sail and on 3 December it received confirmation of its orders to proceed.

The linking element in at least the first four points was Yamamoto. The plan to attack the American Fleet at its Pearl Harbor base was his. Though he drew his ideas from many sources and much of the detailed planning fell to Commander Minoru Genda, it was first and foremost Yamamoto's plan. It was Yamamoto who first formulated the concept and then forced it through to acceptance despite

Below left: As Chief of the Japanese Naval Staff, Rear Admiral Osami Nagano was responsible for the formulation of naval strategy.
Bottom: Rear Admiral Takajiro Onishi took a leading part in planning the Pearl Harbor raid.
Below: Among Japan's newest aircraft carriers in December 1941 was *Shokaku.*

Left: The carrier *Akagi* was launched in 1925 and underwent modernization in 1938. She is pictured during training for the Pearl Harbor strike in the summer of 1941.

opposition from many quarters. He did this because he considered it absolutely essential to Japan's conduct of a war against the Americans. Without his ruthless determination the plan would certainly have been shelved.

It is unclear when Yamamoto first considered the possibility of attacking Pearl Harbor. It may well have been the time when American exercises involving carrier-aircraft attacks on shore installations were carried out in the interwar period. The most notable of these exercises were those of 1932 and 1938, when Pearl Harbor itself was the target of attack, and both maneuvers were deemed to have ended with success for the carrier aircraft. Yamamoto, who made his reputation as an advocate of air power and was one of the very few senior admirals in any navy to wear pilot's wings, cannot have been unaware of these exercises. What is known for certain is that from the time he took up his appointment as Commander in Chief, Combined Fleet Yamamoto showed an extremely keen interest in Pearl Harbor and pushed through a series of measures which, in retrospect, might suggest that he was thinking of a preemptive attack on Pearl Harbor long before November 1940.

Almost as soon as he hoisted his flag his cabin in the *Nagato* housed specially marked maps and intelligence summaries of Pearl Harbor. As the months passed and American activity on Oahu increased so too did the amount of information at Yamamoto's fingertips. It is difficult to believe that this interest was merely casual. On taking up his appointment Yamamoto secured the agreement of the Naval General Staff to widen the Marianas–Carolines war zone to include the Marshalls. In view of the increasing range and speed of aircraft this amendment to Japanese plans was prudent, but Yamamoto used it as the first step in the extension of the war zone right up to Pearl Harbor itself. This, again, was sensible, though it was done without any commensurate increase in auxiliary vessels needed to make such an extension workable. An enemy coast is always one's own first line of defense, but Yamamoto's proposals were more than a recognition of the truth of this simple dictum. He planned to use submarines off Hawaii – an idea that accorded with Japanese use of 'cheap craft, capable of quick and easy replacement' at the forward edge of the battle area. The point is, however, that aircraft also fell into this category.

On his appointment Yamamoto also began to draw back naval aircraft and aircrew from China. Owing to their superior range over their army counterparts, naval aircraft were much in demand in China. Yamamoto began to recall naval aircraft and started a program of retraining crews for attacks on shipping – a very different proposition from attacks on land objectives. In April and May 1940, at Yamamoto's insistence, a series of war games was played involving attacks by carrier aircraft on shipping anchored in harbor. The results of these games were naturally open to dispute, but two general conclusions cautiously emerged. The first was that the torpedo would be the most effective weapon with which to attack anchored shipping. The second was that such attacks could prove decisive because moored ships could not evade a torpedo attack. Yamamoto argued a further point from these conclusions. He insisted that if surprise was achieved the results would, not could, be decisive.

Yamamoto's views were to be proved correct in November 1940 when a group of obsolete British carrier aircraft, far inferior to anything that the Japanese possessed, sank or severely damaged three Italian battleships at their moorings in Taranto Harbor. For the loss of just two aircraft the

Right: Japanese pilot selection and training standards were rigorous and exacting. Trainees are shown demonstrating their physical fitness.
Below: Trainees were prepared for the disorientation of aerobatic flying in the crude but effective contraption shown.

British decisively altered the balance of naval power in the Mediterranean. The lesson of the attack was there for all to see – carrier aircraft, attacking with the advantage of surprise, could achieve strategically decisive results. That month, after the attack, Yamamoto spoke for the first time of his idea of using carrier aircraft to attack the US Pacific Fleet at its Pearl Harbor base.

The first man Yamamoto consulted about his plan was his Chief of Staff, Admiral Shigeru Fukudome. Fukudome was unimpressed, and remained skeptical until the time he left the Combined Fleet in October 1941. In deference to his admiral he advised Yamamoto to consult Rear Admiral Takijuro Onishi, then Chief of Staff to the land-based XIth Air Fleet, and one of the most aggressive air-minded officers in the Imperial Navy. Onishi had already toyed with the idea of an attack on Pearl Harbor with aircraft. He had considered using land-based aircraft from the Marshalls, but he had had to abandon the idea because of the insurmountable distance problems involved. Onishi warmed to Yamamoto's idea, but his enthusiasm cooled distinctly with time. He suggested that they consult Genda, one of the ablest staff officers in the Navy. Genda was a firm believer in the value of air power, and he had been attaché in London at the time of the Taranto attack. He was privy to many aspects of the attack. After an initial consideration of Yamamoto's ideas, Genda told the admiral that the plan to attack Pearl Harbor was difficult, but not impossible.

Genda, however, immediately demolished two of Yamamoto's main proposals for an attack. Yamamoto singled out American battleships as the main objective of the attack. It has been suggested that Yamamoto considered the breaking of American battleship strength to be more psychologically devastating than attacks on carriers. Genda thought that this was nonsense. Either carriers were the decisive strike weapon at sea or they were not. If they were, then there could be no justification for using them against lesser weapons or secondary objectives. Genda firmly fixed attention on the main objective of the attack – the elimination of American aircraft carriers.

Genda also refuted Yamamoto's suggestion to use attacking aircraft on a one-way mission. Such an idea might appear ridiculous – though in keeping with Japanese ideas of expendable light units – but Yamamoto had good reasons for such a proposal. Land-based reconnaissance aircraft could sweep the seas around Pearl Harbor to a distance of up to 800 miles, far beyond the range of carrier aircraft. The carriers could not risk being compromised or advancing to a position where they could be counterattacked easily by shore-based aircraft. Using aircraft on a one-way mission and leaving submarines to pick up ditched aircrew would lessen the risks to the carriers. Genda would have none of this. For an attack on Pearl Harbor only the elite of the navy's aircrew could be used, and to risk losing them on the first operation of a war was a luxury Japan could not afford. Such a proposal was certain to be bad for morale, and writing off the aircrew would leave the carriers hopelessly vulnerable if a counterattack materialized. Genda argued that the risks of being compromised had to be accepted but that every effort had to be made to reduce the risks to a minimum.

Genda laid down three conditions for success. He calculated that at least 300 aircraft would have to be used in an attack – making it by far the greatest carrier operation ever carried out – and that this would involve the use of six fleet carriers and eight oilers. This would involve waiting until after the summer of 1941 when the new carriers *Shokaku* and *Zuikaku* entered service. This in fact fitted into Japanese preparations very well. The total mobilzation of the Imperial Navy had been ordered in October 1940, and this would not be complete until November 1941. As the new carriers would not be ready until that time Genda's condition posed no technical problem. Genda also insisted that only the very best aircrews should be selected for the operation and that security and surprise were absolutely essential to success.

Yamamoto accepted these points and Genda, with a very small team of officers, was charged with the drawing up of a plan of attack. Genda worked quickly, the draft was completed in March 1941. By May the final proposals were completed, but some of the technical problems Genda encountered were not solved until November. The problems involved in the operation fell into three main groups: those of the advance-to-contact phase (the time between the carriers leaving port and the aircraft taking off), the technical problems of armory, and the plan of attack itself once the aircraft reached their objective.

The advance-to-contact phase posed the most difficulties because so much had to be left to chance. The problem was the selection of a route to Hawaii and a flying-off point that would run the least risk of detection. Intelligence work, mainly based on radio intercepts, quickly established that American aircraft reconnaissance patrols concentrated on the waters west, south and east of Hawaii – along the major trade routes – but left northern waters relatively free from surveillance. An approach north of Hawaii recommended itself to the Japanese. By passing between Midway and the Aleutians – but out of range of patrols from both – the Japanese would have to sail some stormy and inhospitable waters, unfrequented by merchantmen. The bad weather conditions prevailing in the northern Pacific in the autumn and winter, when fog alternated with bad weather fronts that closed Hawaii from the north and northeast, would provide cover for the Japanese advance. These same rough conditions threatened refuelling and were certain to cause major navigational problems and difficulties in station keeping and time keeping. The final plan had a hairline schedule because it had to be synchronized with other operations; the Japanese could not afford delays. The carriers would have to refuel once and their escorts at least twice during their mission, and in the stormy north Pacific this would be difficult. Careful research, however, which included a liner, the *Taiyo Maru*, sailing most of the proposed route in October 1941, revealed that on seven days in a month weather conditions moderated sufficiently to permit refuelling at sea. These were not good odds but Genda and Yamamoto had to accept them because there was no alternative.

The technical problems involved in the plan to attack Pearl Harbor were formidable, but most of them were solvable. Most of the problems centered around the torpedo, accepted by Genda as the primary means of attack. Japanese aerial torpedoes were designed to be dropped at about 250 feet and at speeds of up to 150 knots. They generally plunged to about 14 fathoms before running to their required depth. They needed to run some 600 feet in water before arming themselves. Clearly there were problems because Pearl Harbor drew no more than eight fathoms and conventional torpedoes would run themselves harmlessly into the bed of the harbor unless they were modified. Moreover, the greatest expanse of water between the shoreline and where the Americans habitually anchored their capital ships was no more than 1600 feet – which represented less than six seconds of flight for a torpedo bomber. The amount of space and water available for a torpedo run was therefore much less than 1600 feet, and this posed obvious problems. In addition, the American practice of mooring ships in pairs meant that the ship standing out toward the deep water channel shielded its landward neighbor from torpedo attack. Obviously, torpedoes by themselves would not be enough.

These problems forced two considerations. Firstly, modifications to the torpedoes had to be made. The British attack at Taranto, in waters of eight fathoms, showed that there was a solution to this problem. Secondly, bombs would have to be used against the inner targets. These bombs would have to be much larger and more powerful than conventional bombs if they were to inflict telling damage on massive armored heavy ships.

The bomb problem proved relatively easy to settle. New armor-piercing bombs, weighing up to 1600 pounds and based on shells, could be fitted with special fins to give stability and enhanced penetrative powers. Such bombs were quickly manufactured, but new torpedoes could not be quickly improvised. It was not until September that tests were concluded and production started on torpedoes equipped with wooden fins which seemed capable of keeping the weapon shallow-running. Even then only an 80 percent efficiency rating was given to these weapons. The production run to meet the requirements of the Pearl Harbor attack was not complete until mid-November. One of the carriers involved in the operation, the flagship *Akagi*, had to wait behind to collect the full quota of torpedoes after the rest of the carriers had left for their operational base.

Even these torpedoes presented problems. In order to prevent them from diving deep they had to be launched by a bomber flying at about 50 feet above the sea at approximately 150 knots. Pilots would have to be trained to meet these exacting requirements, but with turbulence off the sea and the height of waterside buildings both in the practice areas and at Pearl Harbor, the requirements exacted by the torpedoes broke every safety regulation in the Imperial Navy's training manuals. After crossing the shoreline the bombers would have about three seconds to line up on their objectives and deliver their attack before having to bank steeply upward and to the right in order to prevent congestion over the objectives.

Over a period of months, however, the aircrew selected for this operation reached the required standard. It is no exaggeration to assert that the Japanese carrier pilots committed to the raid on Pearl Harbor represented the best-trained aircrew in the world at that time.

At an early stage in the planning Yamamoto selected Kagoshima Bay in southern Kyushu as the training area for aircrews. The bay, with its restricted waters, volcanic island and waterside buildings, bore a strong resemblance to Pearl Harbor. It was selected for precisely that reason.

The bomber crews exercised over Kagoshima Bay for weeks. The torpedo bombers,

perhaps the most vulnerable of the attacking aircraft, were subjected to approach runs through the buildings of Kagoshima before a flight at 50 to 70 feet above the waters of the bay. By the end of October the bombers were making up to four runs a day. The dive bombers, meanwhile, had their release point lowered from 2000 feet to 1500 feet to increase the prospect of securing a hit while the high-level bombers – whose accuracy record in China was low because of their poor quality bombsights – were intensively trained. To offset the weakness of equipment the Japanese had to rely on experience and instinct on the part of the aircrew. To try to achieve the best possible result the Japanese instituted 'pattern bombing.' This is the process by which a tight-flying formation drops its bombs on the signal of a lead aircraft which is manned by the best and most experienced crew available. In this way the Japanese could reasonably expect to achieve a very tight grouping and therefore a high rate of strikes. Against moving targets the pilots achieved an estimated 80 percent hit rate by the time their training was complete. When in September the aircrews were directed to train against anchored ships there was a general sense of anticlimax. Attacks on stationary targets as opposed to targets at sea were regarded as obviously less important, but when the purpose of their training change was revealed the aircrews responded. The final exercise of 6 November involved a 200-mile flight from the carriers to the targets in Kagoshima Bay, and it is evident that the results gave even Yamamoto cause for satisfaction.

The dictum 'Train Hard, Fight Easy' was to be fully borne out by the attack on Pearl Harbor, but much of the smooth running of the attack stemmed from Genda's care and attention to detail. All through the training phase the aircrew had to meet Genda's two basic demands. They had to be able to recognize enemy ships correctly and at a glance, and then line up on their objectives. They had to know exactly what they had to do and how it was to be achieved. There was no room for error; every bomb and every torpedo had to count. In the congested airspace over the objective pilots had to keep to very exact battle drills if they were not to mask the attacks of other types of aircraft. The attacks themselves had to be staggered in order to allow the different types of aircraft to mount their attacks under the most favorable conditions possible. The final problem Genda faced was the tricky one of devising a recovery program that would allow Japanese aircraft to regain their carriers without leading surviving American forces against the carrier task force.

There were many technical details to be settled when Genda presented his final proposals, but in all operational aspects the plan was complete. In November, the morning of Sunday 7 December (Hawaiian time) was selected for the attack. The best hope of favorable weather conditions, suitable for refuelling, came in the first half of December when moon conditions for the final night run to Pearl Harbor would be most favorable. A Sunday was selected because this was the time best to catch the Americans unprepared.

The final plan of attack involved two quite distinct operations. There was to be a strike by carrier aircraft and there was to be a major submarine effort off Hawaii. The first operation involved a task force of six fleet carriers, two battleships, two heavy cruisers and a light screen of one light cruiser and nine destroyers from the 1st Destroyer Flotilla. With this force sailed eight oilers. Two more destroyers were in company but these were detailed for the simultaneous bombardment of American installations on Midway. Three fleet submarines were detailed to scout the route of the task force. The second part of the attack involved no less than 27 submarines – 11 of which carried reconnaissance aircraft – with all but two detailed to take up their stations off Hawaii. The submarine force thus deployed represented nearly 42 percent of the entire submarine service. (For a full order of battle, and the fate of all the Japanese ships that took part in the attack see Appendix.)

The carrier task force was to sail from its remote anchorage at Tankan Bay in the Kuriles and make its way at 13 knots – the most economical cruising speed of the heaviest carriers *Akagi* and *Kaga* and the escorting destroyers – to a position some 500 miles north of Oahu by the evening of 6 December. Then, leaving the oilers to make for a preselected rendezvous, the force was to make a high-speed run through the night to be in its flying-off position about 260 miles north of Oahu by dawn. The task force was given strict instructions to abandon its mission if it was recalled or if it was compromised before 6 December. If the force was detected on the 6th the force commander, Vice-Admiral Chuichi Nagumo, was given discretion to continue or abandon the mission. British, American and Dutch merchantmen encountered en route were to be sunk. Other nationals were to be boarded and their radios rendered inoperative.

From its flying-off position the force would launch two strikes, one hour apart. Both strikes were to consist of slightly under 200 aircraft. Some 80 aircraft were to be held back for combat air patrol and as a reserve. The two attacking waves would attack the six air bases the Japanese believed were on Oahu – in fact there were seven – and the warships in the anchorage. If surprise was achieved the attack would be led by the torpedo bombers and followed by the high-level bombers and then the dive bombers. Fighters and dive bombers would spearhead the attack if surprise was lost. As there was a chance that major American units – either Admiral Pye's battle line or Admiral Halsey's mixed carrier-battleship force – might not be in harbor at the time of the attack, the bombers were to search up to 150 miles south of Oahu in an effort to gain contact. The recovery phase involved aircraft breaking off contact and flying south before reversing course and sweeping wide of Oahu to regain their carriers. This was ordered in an effort to mislead the Americans over the true whereabouts of the carriers. The carriers were to maintain radio silence at all times and were not to take any steps to help the aircrews regain their ships.

The submarines were to sail before the carrier force either from Japan via Kwajalein or directly from Kwajalein itself. Two submarines were detailed to scout the Aleutians and Samoa, but the remaining 25 were deployed off Oahu. From Yokosuka the 1st and 2nd Flotillas deployed four submarines to the north and seven submarines to the east of Oahu respectively. From Kwajalein nine submarines of the 3rd Flotilla took up station to the south of the island. The 1st Flotilla was to be joined on patrol by Nagumo's three submarines after they had led the way for the task force while the submarines lined up south of Pearl Harbor were to be joined by five submarines which were detailed to carry two-man midget submarines to Hawaii. These midget submarines, armed with two torpedoes, were to break into Pearl Harbor and rest on the bottom throughout the 7th. At dusk they were to carry out attacks on surviving American units. Their parent submarines were charged with recovering the midgets off Lanai, though there was little hope of this. These five fleet submarines, when they joined the 3rd Flotilla, were to undertake operational patrols designed to secure intelligence, rupture American lines of communication between the Hawaiian Islands and the United States and to deplete American strength by dealing with any warships that attempted to break out of Pearl Harbor during and after the attack. Many naval officers who were skeptical of the carrier part of the operation entertained great hopes of the submarines which would be operating in the orthodox fleet role for which they had been designed and

Left: The commander of the carrier task force which attacked Pearl Harbor was Vice Admiral Chuichi Nagumo, flying his flag in *Akagi*.
Below: Hostilities opened on 7 December when a midget submarine was sunk in the approaches to Pearl Harbor by the minesweeper USS *Condor*.

Bottom: A group photograph, showing senior officers of the US, Japanese, British, French and Italian navies, taken aboard a Japanese flagship in Chinese waters in 1932.

trained. Some expected that the major part of any success would be accomplished by the submarines.

When Yamamoto put forward his detailed proposals in May to the Naval General Staff he encountered a lukewarm reception. There was very little enthusiasm at all for a plan many regarded as a desperate and almost wild gamble.

Part of the resistance Yamamoto encountered was of an institutional or personal nature. He had made many enemies, and many felt that his plan was an attempt to arrogate the devising of strategy to himself. As the weeks slipped away – and American–Japanese relations deteriorated with alarming rapidity – opposition to the Pearl Harbor plan crystallized into five major objections, none of which could be lightly dismissed.

The whole *raison d'être* of the plan revolved around Yamamoto's belief that a war with the Americans was inevitable and that Japan had to launch a preemptive attack on American resources if she was to have any hope of success in the war. This was not fully accepted by many officers in the Imperial Navy, but this doubt was eroded gradually over a few months. After the Japanese occupation of southern Indo-China, the United States, closely followed by the British and Dutch, imposed an

embargo on Japanese trade in oil and steel in July 1941 and the possibility of war with the United States hardened into near certainty. Japan could only watch as her strength drained away, ebbing as each barrel of oil was used up out of her strategic reserve. At the very most Japan's reserves would be good for two years of war and her stockpiles of high-grade aviation fuel were sufficient for just six months of sustained operations. Unless Japan was able to find alternative supplies of oil very quickly or was able to get the three allied nations to lift their embargo, the Japanese knew that they would soon become too weak to do anything other than accept American terms for a resumption of trade between the two countries. The American terms involved the Japanese evacuation of Indo-China and China and their commitment to peaceful methods of adjusting relations between states. No Japanese government could accept such terms. Too much prestige, money and blood had been invested in the China venture. A lame acceptance of such terms would certainly have provoked mutiny and civil war inside Japan, and as her acid test Japan preferred to fight a foreign as opposed to a civil war. However, there were many officers in the Imperial Navy, such as Osami Nagano, who were appalled by the prospect of a war with the United States and who hoped that some means could be found to avoid it. People such as the Chief of the Naval General Staff were prepared to accept virtually any formula to avoid war, but in the last resort they were not prepared to accept the terms the Americans insisted on imposing.

Nagano fixed his argument on two major points. Firstly, every effort had to be made to find a peaceful means of resolving Japan's difficulties – but diplomacy in the autumn of 1941 merely served to show how irreconcilable were the differences between Japan and the United States. Secondly, he argued that there was no overwhelming or imperative need for the Japanese to attack the Americans at all; a war with the British and Dutch in Southeast Asia need not necessarily involve the Americans. There was much to be said for attacking the European empires and trusting that isolationist opinion inside the United States would be strong enough to prevent an American countermove. To Nagano it was inconceivable that President Roosevelt would be able to lead the Americans into a war over Malaya, the Indies or Siam; this was probably a correct analysis. In many ways the attack on Pearl Harbor came as a relief to the Roosevelt administration because it ended all kinds of problems for it. The issue of how to oppose Japanese aggression and the problem of securing public support for firm action were both resolved in their entirety.

Nagano's argument could be brushed aside with ease. If American hostility toward Japan was such as to ensure American participation in a war at some time or another, then an attack on Pearl Harbor was the best means of ensuring that American involvement came at a time of Japan's choosing and under the most favorable conditions possible for Japan. The Yamamoto formula was simplistic, but effective. The Americans alone were capable of resisting Japan's plans of expansion and their hostility was assured, therefore they had to be crippled at the outset of a war.

With this argument Yamamoto was able to disarm another major criticism of his proposals. It was argued that Japan should seize Southeast Asia before turning to face the Americans in the Marshalls–Carolines–Marianas war zone where the decisive battle to decide the fate of the Empire would be fought. This, of course,

Above: President Franklin D Roosevelt with members of his cabinet aboard the cruiser USS *Indianapolis* in New York Harbor, during a fleet review in May 1934.

was thoroughly in keeping with Japan's prewar planning. Yamamoto's argument pointed to the prospect of shattering American power before such an eventuality arose – in effect Yamamoto was prescribing preventive rather than remedial medicine. If the Americans did sortie to the relief of the Philippines or attempt a reduction of the Marshalls, then an attack on Pearl Harbor would be a broken-back affair, made under crippling handicaps. With the certain knowledge of the implications of the Two-Ocean Act gnawing away at the backs of their minds, Japanese naval officers could not but be impressed by the possibilities opened up by the idea of a surprise attack on Pearl Harbor.

Nevertheless, even those who began to feel the hypnotic effect that all great operations cast over those involved in them had good reason to be apprehensive about various aspects of the planned operation. A carrier strike on Pearl Harbour would remove all the carriers from the crucial area of operations in Southeast Asia. This division of force in the face of an enemy was a dangerously rash policy. What was not realized by proponents of this argument – and what the Americans and British failed to appreciate – was the manner in which Yamamoto and his associates proposed to use long-range shore-based aircraft to make good the absence of the carriers. The Planning Bureau of the Naval General Staff accepted this, however, and devised its war plans in the summer of 1941 on the assumption that the carriers would not be available for operations in Southeast Asia – long before the plan of attack on Pearl Harbor was accepted by Nagano. Yamamoto could not argue this point rationally in defense of his plan. The use of land-based naval aircraft to provide air cover for major naval operations had never been tested. There was no answer to the doubts that arose on such matters as the desperately tight schedule of the carrier force, its possible refuelling problems, its vulnerability to detection and the possibility of heavy loss without commensurate gain. To these points Yamamoto had no effective answer. Detailed planning and intelligence could lessen the risks, but they could not eliminate the elements of chance altogether. Even such people as Onishi began to waver at this point. He had originally estimated a 60 percent chance of success for the proposed operation, but by September he had become decidedly more pessimistic. He came to accept the 40 percent chance assessed by Fukudome.

Indeed, the omens were not too good. In war games held in September to test the whole of the Pearl Harbor concept the first result was a 50 percent loss rate among the Japanese carriers. In the second game the loss rate was 33 percent. At Yamamoto's insistence the games were replayed until Yamamoto gained the result he wanted – decisive success for no loss – which seems a highly unsatisfactory manner of devising strategy. What clinched the argument for Yamamoto was not merely his own personal prestige and authority or his confidence in his plan or the merits of the plan itself – it was the nature of American demands. By October the negotiations between Japan and the United States were clearly floundering, and there seemed no way of avoiding an open break with the Americans. The Japanese came to believe that there was no option but to resort to arms; it naturally followed from this that the American fleet had to be eliminated.

Below left: The Mitsubishi A5M Claude carrier fighter had been largely superseded by the same manufacturer's A6M Zero at the outbreak of war in 1941.
Right: The Japanese navy's Aichi D3A Val dive bomber distinguished itself at Pearl Harbor.
Below right: The army's Nakajima Ki-49 Helen enjoyed little success.
Below: The army's Nakajima Ki-43 Oscar was a near-contemporary of the Mitsubishi A6M Zero.

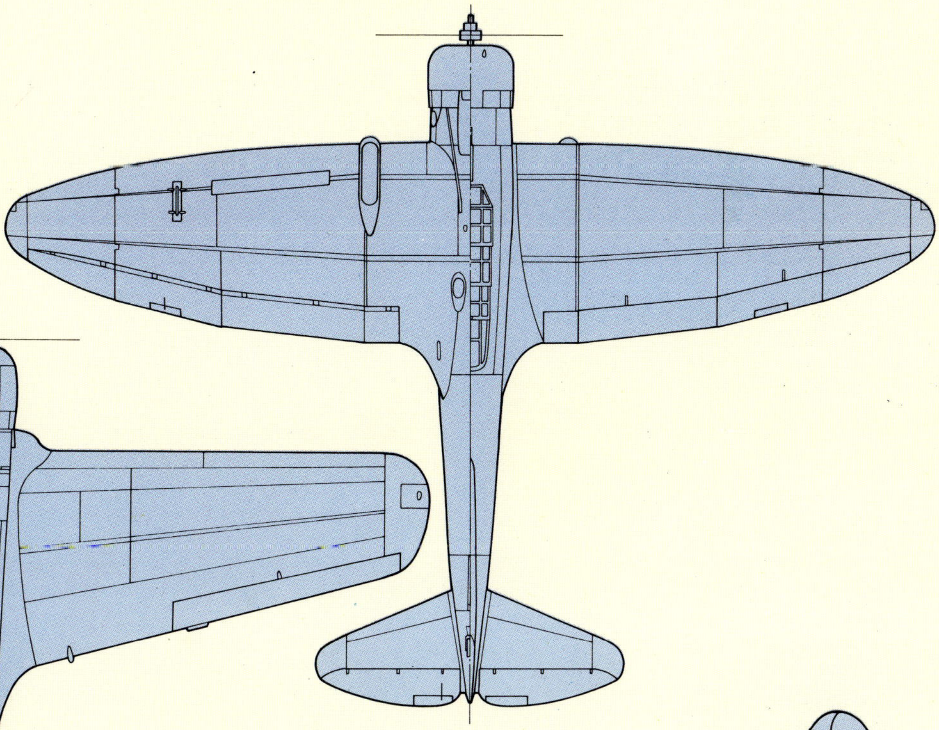

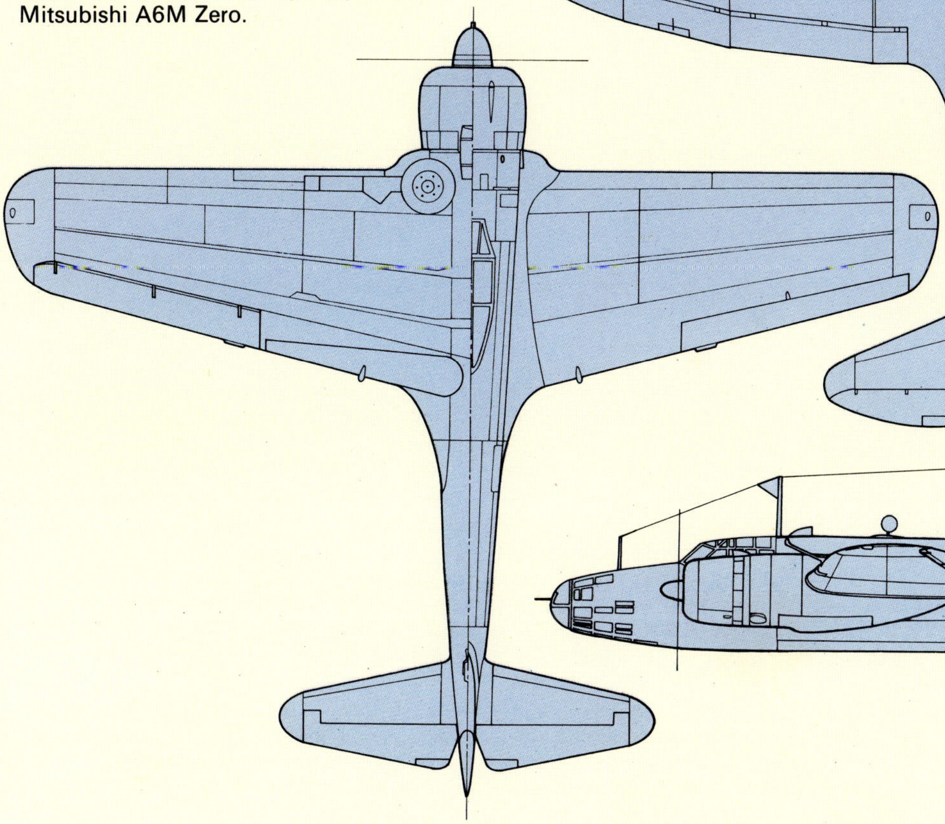

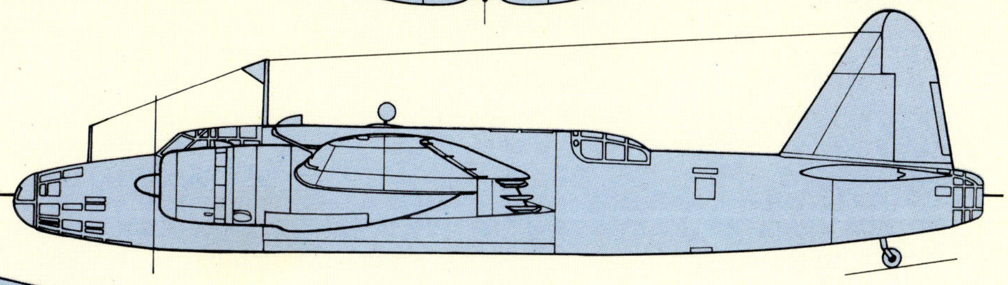

3. THE APPROACH OF WAR

Left: General Hideki Tojo, Japan's war minister, leaves Tokyo by train. The dove of peace emblem is an ironic motif for the man who impelled Japan into the war.

Above: Aircraft parts are dispatched from store.
Above left: A Japanese assembly worker in an aircraft factory.

Field Marshal Slim, writing of Burma, noted that Japan secured the initiative, and hence her early easy victories, 'fairly and inevitably, by paying for it by preparation.' This is certainly true of the Pearl Harbor attack, and perhaps the only apt comment is that the care and attention the Japanese lavished on their plan was not matched by the final result – through no fault of the Japanese themselves.

Ironically, however, for all their efforts the Japanese attack might well have come to nought. The Americans could point to certain developments that clearly pointed to the critical state of American–Japanese relations, and they might well have taken certain measures that would have frustrated the attack. Throughout the summer of 1941 the tone of the Japanese press and radio was strident. The replacement of Prince Konoye by the militantly aggressive General Hideki Tojo as Prime Minister in October 1941 was correctly interpreted as a sign that the war party was in control in Tokyo. Moreover, on 1 December the Imperial Navy changed its codes and it was obvious that this was no routine security precaution. The codes had already been changed on 1 November. To change codes twice in a matter of a month could only point to a need for a very high level of security, far above normal requirements. It could only mean that the Imperial Navy was moving to its battle stations.

The Americans were aware of all these ominous developments, but they also had to hand a whole host of information, much of which served to confuse rather than enlighten. The most productive source of reliable information and intelligence came from Operation Magic. Magic was the name given to the most secret of all American clandestine operations at that time. The Americans had broken the most sensitive of the Japanese diplomatic and naval codes and as a result could read most of the signals between Tokyo and major Japanese embassies and consulates throughout the world.

From Magic the Americans obtained three important pieces of information. They knew that the Japanese had set a deadline of 25 November – later put back four days – for diplomacy to achieve results; if it failed to find a solution, then 'things will automatically begin to happen.' The Americans were also aware that the Japanese had prepared an elaborate series of weather reports – called the wind codes – to warn their people abroad of war or the severing of relations with certain countries. On 4 December the Americans became aware that the Japanese had used the codes relating to their relations with the United States. By then the US had discovered that the Japanese embassy in Washington had been ordered to present a major note to the Secretary of State, Cordell Hull, on 7 December. With a few hours to spare, Magic revealed the content of the note, and the Americans correctly regarded it as tantamount to a declaration of war. Yet with all these warnings they were still caught unprepared by the Japanese attack.

The manner in which the Americans were taken by surprise at Pearl Harbor is often regarded as amazing, but such a view is hardly fair. It is quite easy to see all the warning signs after the event, but it is not so easy to correctly evaluate and interpret – and then decisively act upon – hard intelligence in the midst of a deluge of ambiguous information. In the first week of December the United States knew that war was a matter of hours or days away, but they did not know who was to be attacked and where. They lacked the means to translate the warning, 'War Imminent,' into 'Planned Attack on Pearl Harbor.'

In the autumn of 1941 the Americans

Three scenes in a factory producing land-based bombers for the Japanese navy. The main types built were the Mitsubishi G3M Nell and G4M Betty, the former type being responsible for sinking HMS *Repulse* and HMS *Prince of Wales* off Malaya in 1941.

seriously considered the likeliest target of any Japanese move to be the Maritime Provinces of the USSR. In the light of the German victories in the Soviet Union at this time and the known antagonism between the Japanese and Soviets, such an attack was a distinct possibility and the American assessment was not unreasonable. By November the Americans had revised their assessment, and correctly assumed that the main Japanese effort would be in Southeast Asia. They had no reason to assume that this effort would necessarily involve attacks on American possessions – just as Nagano had argued. If, however, the Japanese did move against the Americans then the likelihood was that they would attack the Philippines – yet even in this move there would be comfort of a kind for Pearl Harbor. American airfields in central Luzon were wrongly believed to be beyond the range of Japanese aircraft in Formosa. If the Japanese, therefore, were to move on the south and if they were to attack the Philippines then they had to use their carriers – hence there was no need to be concerned over the safety of Pearl Harbor. The carriers themselves were assumed to be in Japanese home waters. In fact the Americans by the beginning of December had no idea where the Japanese carriers were. This did not cause any real concern to the Americans; it had happened in the past and the Americans had always relocated the carriers in their home waters when the carriers switched from low frequencies, which the Americans could not find, to their normal high frequencies. This was almost a routine pattern; the Americans had lost and then found the Japanese carriers 12 times during the summer and autumn of 1941. The loss of contact with the Japanese carriers in November and December 1941 can be seen in retrospect to be absolutely crucial, but at the time it had no undue significance.

Unfortunately for the Americans the same was true of one Magic intercept that might have been taken as a clear sign that the Japanese had some move afoot with regard to Pearl Harbor. On 24 September the Japanese consulate in Honolulu was ordered by Tokyo to provide detailed information regarding American warships in Pearl Harbor. Up until that time the consulate had been instructed to give the strength and composition of American ships on the Oahu station, but after 24 September it was given detailed instructions to report arrivals and departures and the exact location of individual warships when they were at their moorings. The consulate was ordered to furnish information regarding ships moored together and it was given a grid pattern so that various stretches of water in Pearl Harbor could be married up to the warships with no possibility of misunderstanding between Honolulu and Tokyo. The signal, which was decoded by the Americans on 9 October, specifically mentioned just one type of warship in the Pacific Fleet, the carriers.

It is difficult to understand why this information was not properly appreciated. The information sought by Tokyo was necessary only if some form of offensive action against Pearl Harbor was being planned. The almost land-locked nature of the anchorage meant that the most likely form of attack was by carrier aircraft. This conclusion had already been reached by two high ranking American officers at Pearl Harbor. Rear Admiral Patrick Bellinger, the Navy's Air Defense Officer, and Major General Frederick Martin, the commander of USAAF on Oahu, had warned Washington that the Japanese might begin a war with an attack on Pearl Harbour. They estimated that such a raid would be made with six carriers approaching Oahu from

Left: US Navy enlisted men wheel an aircraft torpedo across the deck of USS *Lexington* (CV-2). Her gun armament mounted aft of the island was little used.

Below: USS *Yorktown* (CV-5) displaced 19,800 tons and could steam at 33 knots. Her aircraft complement was 81 machines.

the north. They had reached this joint conclusion from their knowledge of Japanese history, their awareness of their own commands' weaknesses and by the simple expedient of examining the options from Japan's point of view. The two commanders submitted their views to Washington in March 1941 – just at the time Genda was drawing up the plans for an attack – and urged that more radars and aircraft, particularly B-17 Flying Fortresses, should be made available for the defense of Pearl Harbor. Bellinger wanted to extend the search area around Pearl Harbor over a full 360 degrees.

Had these radars and aircraft been forthcoming then the Japanese would not have been able to launch their attack in the manner they did. However, they could not be supplied because the United States did not have the B-17s and radars, and their trained crews, in sufficient numbers to provide all-round defense for Pearl Harbor. Resources for the American services before Pearl Harbor, despite the 1940 measures, were desperately scarce and were being diverted on an ever-increasing scale to the Atlantic in an effort to stave off the defeat of Britain. What resources were available for the Pacific were being built up on the Philippines as part of a deterrent force. The corresponding neglect of Oahu was therefore inevitable, but the real point is that the Americans could not see any threat to Pearl Harbor.

Two factors blinded the Americans to Pearl Harbor's vulnerability. The first, paradoxically, was the presence of the US Pacific Fleet itself. The Americans saw their Pacific Fleet as a deterrent; they failed to see that it could act as a magnet. The Americans could see no reason to defend the fleet. One of the major reasons for this was the very isolation of Pearl Harbor. The generals and admirals on Oahu might feel dangerously exposed, but Pearl Harbor was over 3900 miles from Tokyo Bay. The Americans held similar views to the Japanese regarding distances, battle efficiency and fleet strengths. In 1941 the idea of an attack 4000 miles from a fleet base was simply inconceivable. No one really believed it to be politically or strategically possible.

The prevailing disbelief in such a possibility, the lack of proper means of sifting and evaluating information regarding Japanese intentions and capabilities, and the restricted access of Magic information were instrumental in the ignoring of the last warning the Americans received before 7 December. The warnings that came on the day of the attack were far too late to save a fleet that needed some four hours or more to get to sea. On 2 December the liner *Lurline* docked at Honolulu. In the course of her passage from California the liner picked up a series of radio transmissions that she could not identify. Unknowingly the *Lurline* had stumbled across the one security weakness in Japanese radio discipline. In November the Japanese had stepped up their radio traffic in order to confuse their opponents – though to an extent this was certain to be self-defeating – while at the same time ordering the carriers to observe strict radio silence. When the carrier task force was at sea the transmission equipment on the *Hiei*, the task force's communications center, was dismantled in order to prevent accidents, but in order to allow the destroyers to pick up transmissions from Tokyo the capital ships relayed signals from Tokyo on high frequencies simultaneously on low frequencies. US Intelligence missed this, but the *Lurline* accidentally picked it up. She detected and for some days tracked a force, obviously attempting to disguise its movements, closing on Pearl Harbor from the northwest. The liner reported this to the authorities on Oahu when she docked, but the significance of the information was missed – and with it the last chance of avoiding disaster.

Above: A Mitsubishi A6M Zero fitted with a center-line auxiliary fuel tank starts its takeoff run.
Below: An aerial view of the Pearl Harbor anchorage taken only weeks before the attack.

Right: Aircrew of the USAAF's Seventh Air Force relax on Hawaii's Waikiki beach.

4. TORA! TORA! TORA!

On 25 November Yamamoto, anticipating the failure of last-gasp diplomatic efforts to find a peaceful settlement with the Americans, ordered the carrier task force to sail on its mission the following day. Two weeks earlier some of the submarines in home waters that had been detailed for the attack had begun to sail for Kwajalein. There they refuelled between 18–20 November before continuing their mission, this time in the company of submarines already based on the atoll. In dense fog the carrier force slipped out of its desolate anchorage in the Kuriles on the 26th, the last of the carriers clearing Tankan Bay at about 0900 hours.

The task force steamed eastward, following the 43rd Parallel, into the stormy northern Pacific. It encountered only one merchantman – fortunately Japanese – during its entire mission. It steamed eastward at 13 knots with the six carriers, the *Akagi, Kaga, Hiryu, Soryu, Shokaku* and *Zuikaku*, deployed in two columns of three. The carriers were flanked by the heavy cruisers *Chikuma* and *Tone*, while the battleships *Hiei* and *Kirishima* brought up the rear. Nine destroyers, with the flagship the light cruiser *Abukuma*, were in the van. The oilers tended to straggle; their crews were unfamiliar with the exacting standards of station keeping demanded by the warships and every morning saw the escorts rounding up the scattered oilers.

All signals within the task force were by flag and lamp as the force ran into heavy seas. The price paid in storm damage and men washed overboard – particularly during an attempt to refuel on the 28th – was not small, but it had to be accepted. There was no time to search for drowning sailors. On 2 December the task force received the coded message, *Niitaka yama nobore*, which was the signal that Japan had finally decided upon war and that Nagumo was to proceed with the operation as planned. The next day the wind and sea moderated sufficiently to allow refuelling, and the force crossed the International Date Line, thereby gaining a day. The next day – the 4th by Tokyo time to which all Japanese warships worked irrespective of location, but the 3rd by local time – the force turned to the southeast to begin its approach to Pearl Harbor. For four successive days the warships topped up their fuel tanks before, on the evening of the 6th, they were in a position to drop the five remaining tankers and begin their high-speed run through the night in order to reach their flying-off position by dawn.

By the evening of the 6th the crews of the ships had been addressed by their captains, aboard the *Akagi* by Nagumo himself, and the Imperial Rescript announcing the start of the war was read. Yamamoto's personal message that the fate of the Empire rested upon the success of the operation was impressed upon all hands. To add to the gravity of the hour the most precious heirloom in Japanese naval history – the battle flag flown by the legendary Togo at the battle of Tsu-shima in 1905 – was broken out over the *Akagi*. While all the ceremonial of the occasion was being marked, the crisis of the operation was reached; as the task force neared Hawaii Tokyo informed Nagumo that intelligence reports from Oahu showed that no American carriers were in harbor.

When Nagumo's force sailed the Admiral believed that all six American fleet carriers were on the Pearl Harbor station. Japanese intelligence, however, was faulty. Five, not six, carriers had been in the Pacific, but two, the *Hornet* and *Yorktown*, had been transferred to the Atlantic while the *Saratoga* was off the west coast. The *Enterprise* and *Lexington* had been at Pearl Harbor, but as Nagumo closed on Hawaii both were at sea and their whereabouts were unknown to the Japanese. Following war warnings issued when the Americans believed that the Japanese might begin operations at the end of November – and later when Japanese moves against Southeast Asia were detected – the Americans had decided upon a reinforcement of the Pacific islands. Both the carriers had been ordered to ferry Marine Corps aircraft, the *Enterprise* to Wake and the *Lexington* to Midway.

The absence of the carriers opened up all kinds of possibilities for the Japanese task force, not least the prospect of being compromised and counterattacked. Intelligence reports were reassuring on this matter. There was no sign of any unusual American activity or precautions on Pearl Harbor. The warships were not protected by torpedo nets, which had been rejected on the grounds that they would unduly restrict the deep-water channels, and no barrage balloons were being flown. The commercial radio stations on Hawaii were broadcasting as normal. There was no sign that the Americans had any inkling that the Japanese had divided their forces to attack various targets separated by thousands of miles of ocean.

For Genda and those of similar persuasion the whole point of the attack would be lost if the American carriers escaped unscathed, but the rigidity of the timetable of the attack did not allow the Japanese to wait for them to return. Nagumo's Chief of Staff, Rear Admiral Ryunosuke Kusaka, was not unduly disturbed by the carriers' absence; he considered that the eight battleships at Pearl Harbor – the ninth, the *Colorado*, was undergoing dockyard work on the west coast – were more than equal in value to the absent carriers. Nagumo was not prepared to delay or abandon the plan of attack. It was inconceivable to him that he should hesitate on account of ships that were not at their moorings waiting to be attacked. He could reasonably hope that one carrier at least might return in time to be sunk. The heavy cruisers normally with the *Enterprise* had returned to their moorings, and it was not unreasonable to suppose that the carrier herself might be at her berth on the morning of the attack. To try to locate the missing carriers Nagumo ordered the two heavy cruisers to fly off their reconnaissance aircraft before dawn on the 7th to search Pearl Harbor and the Pacific Fleet's occasional alternative anchorage at Lahaina Roads, Maui. Both places were empty of carriers.

Soon after the cruisers flew off their aircraft and just before dawn on the 7th, the task force reached its flying-off position, 230 miles north and slightly to the east of Pearl Harbor. The carriers turned eastward into a fresh wind, but with a strong southerly sea running conditions for launching aircraft were tricky. Only two aircraft were lost as 183 took to the air in record time. Firstly, the 43 Mitsubishi A6M2 Zero-sen fighters rose to fly combat air patrols as 51 Achi D3A2 Val dive bombers and 89 Nakajima B5N2 Kate level-altitude bombers struggled into formation. Forty Kates, the cutting edge of the attack, carried torpedoes; the other Kates were armed with heavy armor-piercing bombs. As these aircraft rose from the decks of their carriers one thing was clear: the Americans at Pearl Harbor now lacked the time and the means to avoid anything other than a stunning defeat.

The last chance the Americans had of redeeming the situation came and went about 0400 hours when the minesweeper *Castor* made contact with one of the midget submarines as it approached the defenses of the anchorage. The encounter was only fleeting, and the duty destroyer *Ward* failed to obtain contact with the submarine when she came to the assistance of the *Castor*. An unconfirmed contact could not be used to alert the fleet, and when the *Ward* sank two midget submarines at 0645 and 0703 hours with guns and depth charges, it was too late for the American chain of command to appreciate and react to the situation. The destroyer *Helm* was ordered to assist the *Ward* and the *Monaghan* was ordered to stand by to give assistance if necessary, but little more could be done in a situation that seemed to lack urgency.

Similarly, there was a seeming lack of urgency concerning the last warning the Americans received before the first bombs fell. The last chance was provided by the radar station at Opana on the most northerly part of Oahu. The station obtained contact with incoming Japanese aircraft at 0702 and continued to track the first wave until 0739 when the aircraft entered a 'blind spot.' Privates Joseph Lockard and George Elliot reported contact with an extremely large number of aircraft closing Oahu from the north at 150 knots at 0706, but the Duty Officer at the Shafter Information Center, the tactical center for the radar stations on Oahu, misinterpreted the warning. A quite plausible explanation for the contact was possible. With the American carriers at sea the contact could be with aircraft flown home in advance of the carriers. Alternatively, the contact could be with a group of B-17s being flown in from California that morning. As a result of these considerations no precautions were taken – indeed the contact was not even reported to higher authorities. It would have made very little difference if they had been. None of the airfields was fully operational and the fleet could not have cleared harbor in the time that was available. All that could have been achieved was for some of the fighters to get into the air to meet the Japanese. Ammunition could have been broken out on ships and ashore. Japanese casualties would have been much higher than was to be the case, but the overall result could hardly have been changed by such actions.

As the Japanese aircraft came over Oahu the strike leader, Commander Mitsuo Fuchida, had to decide the form of attack. This was no easy task because he had to decide whether or not surprise had been

Above: Admiral Isoroku Yamamoto was Japan's greatest naval tactician and architect of the victory at Pearl Harbor.
Left: Warplanes crowd the flight deck of a Japanese carrier with engines running before takeoff. A6M Zeros are in the foreground, with Val dive bombers behind.
Below: A map of the Hawaiian island of Oahu and a plan of the Pearl Harbor naval base.

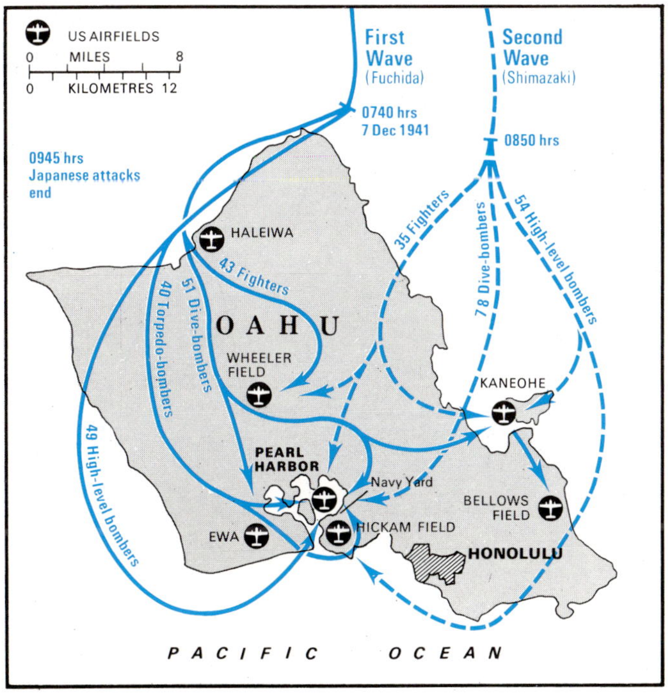

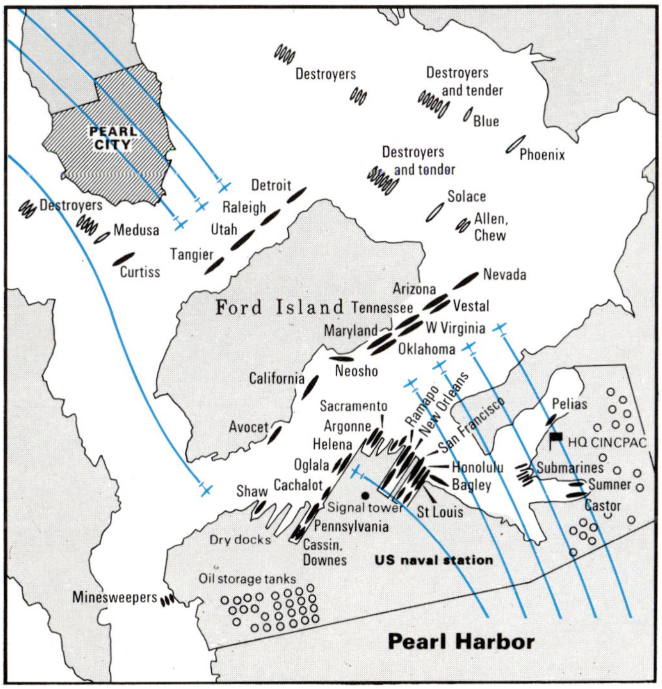

29

Left: Flight-deck crewmen position an A6M Zero for takeoff on 7 December 1941.
Below left: The Zero fighter won an enviable reputation during the early stages of the Pacific War.
Below right: B-17 Flying Fortress bombers parked on Hickam Field during the Japanese attack.
Right: Smoke and flames engulf the headquarters buildings at Hickam Field, the main USAAF airfield on Oahu.

achieved while at 10,000 feet in cloud. At 0740 he decided that surprise had been achieved and he fired one 'Black Dragon' flare to indicate that the torpedo bombers should lead the attack. These bombers immediately broke off to start their approaches, but the fighters missed the signal from Fuchida. He therefore fired another flare for their benefit. Two flares, however, was the signal for 'Surprise Lost' and the dive bombers immediately switched their routine. The result was that Genda's carefully phased plan of attack went by the board, but Fuchida was sufficiently confident of the outcome to transmit the victory signal, *'Tora, Tora, Tora'* at 0753, two minutes before the first bombs fell. Below him in Battleship Row were seven battleships, virtually nose to tail at the moorings. It was a target a novice pilot could hardly miss, and the aircraft that banked into the attack were crewed by anything but beginners.

The first bombs fell on the Naval Air Station on Ford Island in the middle of Pearl Harbor, but in the opening wave Japanese fighters and dive bombers divided their attentions between this airfield and Hickam (US Army bombers), Wheeler and Bellows (US Army fighters), Ewa (US Marine Corps aircraft), Kaneohe Naval Air Station (reconnaissance aircraft) and Schofield Barracks (HQ of the 24th and 25th Infantry Divisions). Although all these airfields were subjected to attack at various times throughout the next two hours, the major part of the damage they sustained was inflicted in the first devastating minutes. Hardest hit were Kaneohe, which lost all 33 of its aircraft in the first assault, and Ewa, which lost 33 of its 49 aircraft in the opening attack. At the end of the day these two fields between them mustered one operational aircraft. At the time of the attack there were 394 aircraft on Oahu of which 139 army and 157 navy aircraft were operational. Of these only 88 were fighters, but such was the fury and violence

Below: The US Navy's shore-based aircraft did not escape the Japanese onslaught. A Catalina flying boat is in the left background, to its right lies a Kingfisher spotter floatplane.
Right: A burned out Curtiss P-40 fighter lies before No 3 hangar on the USAAF's Wheeler Field.
Far right: While the Japanese attack concentrated on the warships and naval installations in Pearl Harbor, airfield targets on Oahu were not neglected, as this blazing hangar attests.

Above: Sailors struggle to beach a blazing PBY at Kaneohe.

Top: This Consolidated PBY Catalina has been burned almost beyond recognition at Kaneohe.
Top right: Beyond the battered tail of a C-47 transport is one of Hickam Field's shattered hangars.

of the assault that only a handful of them were able to try to get into the air to give battle on equal terms. Very few of those that did try to get into the air were successful because most were caught either on their runways or in their initial climbs. Two pilots, Lieutenants Kenneth Taylor and George Welch, did manage to reach their unfinished – and unattacked – army fighter base at Haleiwa, and in three successive missions accounted for seven Japanese aircraft, but otherwise the story was one of unmitigated disaster for the Americans. By the end of the attack most of the airfields had been reduced to ruins, the hangars being singled out for special attention. One hangar at Kaneohe was wrecked by Lieutenant Fusata Iida, the leader of the fighter element of the second wave of attackers. He deliberately crashed his stricken Zero-sen into the hangar after it had been hit by antiaircraft fire, a grim portent of suicide tactics in 1944–45.

By the end of the attack the destruction among the neat rows of parked aircraft, lined up next to the runways in order to minimize the risk of sabotage, was massive. A total of 188 aircraft, almost evenly divided between the army and navy, were completely destroyed. Most were lost on the ground, many as a result of being engulfed in flames as neighboring aircraft were destroyed. Another 159 aircraft, mainly army, were damaged. Among the casualties was one of the 12 B-17s being flown into Oahu that morning. These aircraft arrived at the height of the attack. Most were damaged by Japanese attack, but the sturdiness of the Fortress, plus the lack of firepower in the Zero-sen, ensured that all but one survived. Some of the B-17s even survived extremely hazardous landings on short runways as they sought minor airfields rather than risk attempting to land at Hickam.

Also among the casualties were nine aircraft from the *Enterprise* which were destroyed or damaged by either the Japanese first strike or by American antiaircraft gunners who naturally tended to shoot at anything in the air once they were

Above: Navy men begin salvage operations among burning hangars and PBY flying boats.

Far right: The flame-scarred decks of the battleship USS *Pennsylvania* bear witness to the effectiveness of Japan's Aichi D3A dive bomber.
Right: USS *West Virginia* fell victim to the first attacking wave of Nakajima B5N Kate torpedo bombers.
Below: USS *California* was one of eight battleships sunk at their moorings, yet all but two were later raised and repaired.

YSP 14
YSP 13

Top left: A Japanese photo taken during the attack by Kate torpedo bombers on battleship row at about 0800 hours.
Above left: The result of the attack by the first wave of torpedo bombers can be seen in this Japanese photograph.
Left: Salvage tugs attempt to keep the cruiser *Raleigh* afloat. The capsized hull of USS *Utah* can be seen astern.

Above: The Mitsubishi Ki-21 Sally was one of the Japanese Army Air Force's chief bombers at the start of the Pacific War.
Below: This B-17 Flying Fortress force landed on Bellows Field to escape Japanese fighters. It had arrived on a ferry flight from the United States in the middle of the Japanese attack.

able to come into action. Eighteen aircraft were flown off the *Enterprise* and they arrived over Ford Island at about 0800 hours. The carrier herself had been due back at 0730 but she had been delayed by refuelling problems. At the time of the attack she was some 200 miles west of Oahu, but the sacrifice of her aircraft was not in vain. As her pilots ran into the Japanese attackers over Pearl Harbor warnings were sent to the carrier and the *Enterprise*, observing radio silence, vanished westward into the vastness of the ocean.

For the capital ships in harbor there could be no escape. As the torpedo bombers broke into the attack those on the inside of the turn reached their objectives slightly before their colleagues on the outside. The result was that the warships lined up on the northwest side of Ford Island took the first blows rather than the battleships to the southeast. Five aircraft came over Pearl City against the target battleship *Utah* and the cruisers *Detroit* and *Raleigh* which were anchored in the berths normally used by the carriers. The *Detroit* was missed by her lone assailant, but the *Raleigh* was struck by a single torpedo while the *Utah* took two. Immediately the *Utah*, because she had been decommissioned and lacked the armor protection needed to survive such damage, began to settle to port. One of the attacking Kates, however, held off, skimmed Ford Island and Battleship Row and let fly at the *Oglala* and *Helena*, moored together in the normal berth of the Pacific Fleet's flagship, the *Pennsylvania*. The torpedo passed under the *Oglala* and hit home on the cruiser at precisely 0757 hours. The *Helena* immediately settled but the *Oglala*, a minelayer, was effectively destroyed by concussion. She was 34 years old, and had not been designed as a warship. She was not compartmentalized and literally burst at the seams. It was later alleged that she died of fright, but this was no joke. Her lack of internal structural strength made her subsequent raising the most difficult of the salvage operations undertaken at Pearl Harbor.

It was then the turn of Battleship Row. At 0758 hours the first torpedoes hammered home against the *Oklahoma*, outboard of the *Maryland*, and the *West Virginia*, moored outside the *Tennessee*. The *Arizona*, inboard but unprotected by the repair ship *Vestal*, took two torpedoes in the first attack. In the next few minutes a series of torpedoes hit the hapless *Oklahoma* and *West Virginia*. The *West Virginia* was torn to pieces by perhaps as many as six torpedoes, but miraculously, with all power gone, counterflooding and the strength of the retaining wires held her list to 13 degrees and she settled more or less upright on the harbor bottom. The *Oklahoma* was not so fortunate. Five torpedoes gashed her port side wide open and she began to capsize. Two more torpedoes crashed into her as she began to keel over. By 0806 hours she had gone.

Above: The superstructure of the battleship USS *Arizona* is wreathed in flames and smoke. She later capsized, trapping 400 seamen in her hull.
Below: Another view of *Arizona* showing the explosion of her forward magazine, which showered the harbor with blazing debris.

Left: West Virginia's ensign keeps flying after the attack.
Below left: Nevada was beached on Waipio Point to prevent her sinking at her moorings.

Bottom: USS *Oklahoma*, capsized astern of *Maryland*, could not be salvaged.
Below: The sky above Pearl Harbor was filled with AA bursts.

The *California* was anchored a little apart from the other battleships and made a poor target, but the torpedo bombers knew their business and finished her with just two torpedoes. In normal circumstances the *California* would perhaps have avoided sinking, but her double bottom had been opened up ready for inspection the following day. The sea water rushed unchecked through the ship and she began to settle rapidly. At the other end of the line the *Nevada* took a single torpedo that tore an enormous hole in her port bow, and soon afterward she was struck by two heavy bombs, one of which destroyed the starboard antiaircraft director. Within a matter of minutes of the start of the attack all the battleships in the Row, with the exception of the *Maryland* and *Tennessee*, had been crippled or severely damaged and the scene was set for the first of the three great moments of drama of the attack.

As the torpedo bombers completed their executions, the high-level bombers joined the attack. Not only was the *Nevada* hit but so too was the *West Virginia*. Two bomb hits on the *West Virginia* did massive damage. Her three armored decks forward of the bridge were telescoped together and most of the ship between the forecastle and forward turret was burned out. The two

Despite the devastation wrought by the Japanese, Pearl Harbor recovered from the attack with surprising speed. Six of the eight battleships were returned to service, as were many of the damaged smaller craft.

Left: Smoke billows from the burning USS *Arizona* at the end of the attack.
Below left: US Marines prepare to engage enemy aircraft with their rifles and a 0.5-caliber machine gun. In the background Douglas Devastator torpedo bombers are parked.
Below: USS *Arizona*'s exploding magazine caused such damage that, like *Oklahoma*, she was never salvaged.

battleships so far immune were also hit; both the *Maryland* and *Tennessee* were hit by two bombs apiece. One of the bombs that wrecked the forward areas of the *Tennessee* ripped out the bridge of the *West Virginia*, disembowelling her skipper, Captain Mervyn Bennion. Bennion was only one man, and a moment or two before he was fatally wounded nearly 1100 men had died when at about 0810 hours the *Arizona* was struck by a bomb on her forecastle. It penetrated through to the forward magazine and the battleship blew up in a sheet of flame that climbed hundreds of feet into the air. High above the stricken ship Fuchida's bomber was shaken by a massive shock wave which also swept men off the *Nevada*, *West Virginia* and *Vestal*. The repair ship, already struck by some of the bombs that had been aimed at the *Arizona*, was hurriedly pulled clear of the fiercely burning wreck by a tug.

By the time the *Arizona* had gone the first faltering barrage was being put up by the ships in harbor. Ten critical minutes passed between the first attacks and the first heavy antiaircraft fire, but gradually the barrage became intensive and more effective. The Americans were beginning to react, but at every turn they were fighting a losing battle. Ammunition lockers had to be smashed open, and even then some of the ammunition, dating from 1918, was found to be defective. The chains of the heavy machine-gun ammunition belts frequently broke, and many of the fuses and charges for the heavier antiaircraft ammunition failed to function. In ships where power was lost ammunition had to be passed by hand, often along crazily-tilting passageways. Gun crews, often lacking directional control, were frequently incomplete. Some ships, which were awaiting or undergoing repair, had no guns to fight with as their weapons had been either removed or partially dismantled. The American chain of command completely collapsed, but men fought as best they could, without much regard to the niceties of rank. By the time the American flak began to blacken the skies most of the damage to be inflicted by the Japanese had been incurred, but the Americans could ensure fierce resistance for the 170 aircraft of the second waves – 80 Vals, 54 high-level Kates and 36 Zeros – that were closing on their objectives.

There was a slight lull in the tempo of the attack on the warships between 0815 and 0830 hours, though at this time Bellows Field received some devastating treatment as nine Zero-sens followed a Flying Fortress coming in to land. In fact the second wave was late, but this did not matter much because many of the high-level bombers from the first wave had to make several runs over their smoke-shrouded objectives before they could drop their bombs. Yet even this small lull afforded the Americans little respite because during it they became conscious of the threat of the midget submarines. The *Helm*, which had steamed down the channel at 27 knots rather than the regulation 14 knots as the attack developed, obtained contact with a midget submarine outside the harbor entrance. The submarine survived the subsequent depth charging, but it was badly shaken and never under full control again. She later drifted ashore near Bellows Field and survived an attempt to scuttle her. Her commander, Ensign Sakamaki, survived to become the first prisoner of the Pacific War.

At 0830 hours, however, just as the second wave attack was beginning to develop, the destroyer-minelayer *Breese* sighted another midget submarine – but this time well into the harbor. The repair ship *Medusa* and the aircraft tender *Curtiss* also sighted the intruder, and with warning flags flying from the three ships' yards, the *Monaghan* turned to engage. All four American ships fired at the submarine, which in turn fired at, but missed, the anchored 508-foot long *Medusa* and the onrushing *Monaghan*, which caught the submarine a glancing blow. As the American warships passed over the Japanese boat, the *Monaghan* blew the submarine to pieces with a shallow-pattern depth-charge attack set at 30 feet. The destroyer escaped damage but ran ashore in the very restricted waters of the channel. However, she recovered and was able to reach the sea.

Further back in the harbor the second major incident was unfolding as at the end of Battleship Row the *Nevada* began to get under way. In normal circumstances it took about 3 hours 30 minutes for a battleship to raise steam and be maneuvered into the channel by tugs, but 45 minutes after the start of the attack the *Nevada*, without assistance, began to nose her way into deep water. Those who saw her agreed that one of the most magnificent and awesome sights of the day was the stricken battleship, against a black background of smoke and death, seeking the channel as the wind caught and unfurled the Stars and Stripes over her quarterdeck in a superb gesture of defiance.

As the *Nevada* moved down the channel, with no captain and only a handful of officers aboard, it seemed as if the entire second wave of attackers had the same thought of sinking her in the channel, thereby preventing any warship either

Left: Rescue teams attempt to save survivors from *West Virginia*.
Below left: This rusting hull served to remind American sailors of the 'day of infamy.'

Above: An Aichi D3A Val dive bomber noses over onto its target. Note that its underwing dive brakes are deployed.
Below: A Japanese midget submarine lies beached on a South Pacific island. Craft of this type opened the Pearl Harbor attack.

Above: Japanese bombs raise fountains of water around small craft in Pearl Harbor.

entering or leaving harbor. Dive bombers came at her from every direction, smothering her with a series of hits. Reeling under the impact of these blows and with fires spreading rapidly throughout her, the *Nevada* began to settle lower in the water. The danger of her sinking in the channel was appreciated and as she neared the floating drydock signal flags could be seen at the Naval District Headquarters ordering the *Nevada* to stay clear of the channel. With some reluctance the battleship was run aground at Hospital Point on the southern shore, where she was turned around by the tide to face the way she had come.

The *Nevada* perhaps achieved more than she realized by her abortive sortie. She began to get under way at about 0840 hours and immediately drew enemy aircraft against her. Japanese aircraft paid no attention to the aviation-fuel carrier *Neosho*, anchored between the *California* and *Maryland*, which began to get under way at 0835 hours. Japanese aircraft, intent on greater prey, let her get clear of Battleship Row unmolested. Had the Japanese attacked the *Neosho*, and had she exploded, it is distinctly possible that she would have destroyed three or four battleships. As it was, burning oil from the *Oklahoma* drifted down on the *California* and forced her abandonment at 1002 hours. Fortunately, however, the wind changed and blew the oil clear of the battleship which was quickly reboarded and her many fires, caused by both waves of attackers, were tackled.

With smoke covering so many targets, Japanese aircraft turned on the largest undamaged target remaining. This was the Fleet flagship *Pennsylvania* in Drydock 1010. She was berthed with the destroyers *Cassin* and *Downes*. During the first attack the drydock was flooded to prevent the battleship surging forward and crushing the destroyers if and when the dock gates were destroyed. This also had the effect of raising the battleship level to the dockside, thus allowing her antiaircraft guns to come into action. The flagship was only hit once but the destroyers were hit repeatedly. Even before the dock was flooded both the destoyers were in flames and at 0937 hours the *Cassin* was shaken by a massive blast and she keeled over to starboard and rolled on top of the *Downes*. Just along from the drydock was the destroyer *Shaw* in the floating drydock, and she was also badly hit. Her demise provided the third spectacular moment of the attack. A heavy fire, caused by a bomb hit at 0912 hours, reached her forward magazine at 0930 hours and the forecastle of the destroyers quite literally blew up. Debris, shells and bodies were thrown hundreds of feet into the sky in one awesome explosion.

By the time the *Shaw* exploded the full fury of the Japanese attack had passed, though a few more heavy blows were still to be struck. The *Curtiss* was hit by a bomb and a crashing bomber, and then shaken by a series of near misses. The 8325-ton destroyer-tender *Dobbin* was likewise badly jolted by a near miss that killed an entire gun crew while the *Raleigh* was struck by a bomb that passed through her and exploded in the bed of the harbor. This started a massive improvised operation to keep the cruiser afloat. The *Honolulu* was also caught by a near miss which damaged her oil tanks and warped her armor, but with that the raiders were gone. One last raking over the nearby airfields and it was all over, all except for Fuchida. The attack leader continued to circle for an hour assessing the damage before he, too, turned directly for the carriers. En route he picked up two fighter stragglers and returned them safely to their ships.

In order to help his aircraft return, Nagumo had moved his carriers to within 190 miles of Pearl Harbor, a desperately close distance but one which Nagumo felt was justified by the knowledge that those extra miles closer might make all the difference between recovery and loss of aircraft that were damaged or low on fuel. In all 324 of the attacking aircraft returned, the last being Fuchida at about 1300 hours. Fuchida went straight to Nagumo and Kusaka to report. With rearming and refuelling the aircraft well under way, Fuchida urged Nagumo to mount another assault. Fuchida argued that there were still many suitable targets for an attack and that the American defenses were negligible. He hoped that a second strike might catch one or more of the carriers.

Yamamoto, in the *Nagato* in Kure Harbor, anticipated the course of action that would be adopted. He predicted that Nagumo would withdraw and not renew the attack. Yamamoto knew of Nagumo's chronic doubts about the operation and that the Vice-Admiral had never had much confidence in the plan in the first place. Yamamoto knew that the responsibility of command of the carriers bore heavily on Nagumo and that Nagumo was well aware of the vulnerability of carriers to dive-bomb attacks. It was Nagumo who, in the argument before the attack, had pointed out that the carriers would be exposed along the whole length of their flight decks and vulnerable to attack. It was a fear that was to be realized at Midway in June. As Fuchida argued his case Nagumo hardened in his view that little could be expected from a renewal of the attack; the security of the carriers themselves was his first concern. Kusaka knew his Admiral's mind and at 1330 hours gave the order to begin the withdrawal.

5. THE DAY OF INFAMY

By confirming Kusaka's order Nagumo turned his back on the chance to secure total victory at Pearl Harbor. It was a chance that never came again to the Imperial Navy. Nagumo and Kusaka acted as commanders who had narrowly avoided defeat rather than as admirals who had a devastating strategic victory within their grasp. Admiral Chester W Nimitz, the commander of American naval forces in the Pacific for much of the war, was to comment that the weakness of the Pearl Harbor operation was that it was not sustained. The observation is accurate because it points to the fact that the Japanese were attempting to do too much in a single operational strike. Had the Japanese attempted a selective second and perhaps even a third strike then crippling damage might well have been inflicted. As it was, Nagumo's considered opinion was that despite his fears a major strategic success had been achieved, and that little more could have been attained that would have justified the risks.

Nagumo had good reason to be pleased with the success of the operation. At a cost of 29 aircraft – five Kates, 15 Vals and nine Zero-sens – and all five of the midget submarines, the Japanese sank or severely damaged 18 warships and auxiliaries, wiped out 80 percent of the aircraft on Oahu at the time of the attack, and killed and wounded 3681 American personnel. Nearly half of the 2403 Americans killed were lost in the *Arizona*. To a world that was accustomed to measuring naval power in terms of the number of battleships a nation possessed, Pearl Harbor was an unmitigated disaster. On 6 December 1941 the Americans possessed 17 battleships, nine of which were in the Pacific. By the end of the following day the Americans were left with a mere eight that were fit for operations. Eight had been lost or put out of commission at Pearl Harbor while the *Colorado* was in the naval dockyard at Bremerton, Washington. All that were left were the battleships of the Atlantic Fleet and some of these were rather elderly.

The debacle, however, was nowhere near as bad as first appearances suggest, and it was certainly less severe than it might have been. As the smoke from burning ships and installations billowed over Oahu what was not immediately obvious was the fact that the basic necessities for a successful counteroffensive remained unmolested. Losses were concentrated among the battleships. Grievous though the battleship losses were, with five sunk and three damaged, all

Below: Rescue teams work to release trapped seamen from the capsized hull of USS *Oklahoma*.

Right: The shocked reaction of Americans to the Japanese attack is reflected in the headlines of the *Honolulu Star-Bulletin*.
Below: The Japanese victory at Pearl Harbor was not entirely without cost. American sailors salvage an Aichi D3A shot down during the attack.

Honolulu Star-Bulletin 1st EXTRA

8 PAGES—HONOLULU, TERRITORY OF HAWAII, U. S. A., SUNDAY, DECEMBER 7, 1941—8 PAGES ★ PRICE FIVE CENTS

WAR!

(Associated Press by Transpacific Telephone)

SAN FRANCISCO, Dec. 7.—President Roosevelt announced this morning that Japanese planes had attacked Manila and Pearl Harbor.

OAHU BOMBED BY JAPANESE PLANES

SIX KNOWN DEAD, 21 INJURED, AT EMERGENCY HOSPITAL

Attack Made On Island's Defense Areas

CIVILIANS ORDERED OFF STREETS

ANTIAIRCRAFT GUNS IN ACTION

BOMB NEAR GOVERNOR'S MANSION

HOUR OF ATTACK—7:55 A. M.

CITY IN UPROAR

Hundreds See City Bombed

Names of Dead and Injured

Schools Closed

Editorial

COURTESY: PACIFIC MERCANTILE LIMITED

Honolulu Star-Bulletin 2nd EXTRA

8 PAGES—HONOLULU, TERRITORY OF HAWAII, U. S. A., SUNDAY, DECEMBER 7, 1941—8 PAGES ★★ PRICE FIVE CENTS

DEATHS OVER 400 ON OAHU, LATEST REPORT

TOKYO ANNOUNCES "STATE OF WAR" WITH U. S.

Japanese Raids On Guam, Panama Are Reported

Oahu Blackout Tonight; Fleet Here Moves Out to Sea

Four Waves, Start At 7:55, Oahu Hit In Many Places

Governor Proclaims National Emergency

REPORTS GUAM, PANAMA ATTACKED

Known Oahu Casualties

BULLETINS

Blackout For Oahu Ordered

Inter-Island Ships, Planes Are Held Up

Military Censorship On All Messages

Two Japanese Fliers Captured

Editorial

HAWAII MEETS THE CRISIS

these capital ships were old and slow. They were unable to give battle with the latest German and Japanese battleships on equal terms, and they were too slow to operate efficiently with the fleet carriers. Indeed, in a roundabout manner the loss of the battle line at Pearl Harbor was a blessing in disguise for the Americans, not least because it released survivors from the sunken ships for service in other warships at a time when trained manpower was desperately scarce in the US Navy.

In common with other major navies, the US Navy in the interwar period had been divided on the issue of the relative merits of battleships and aircraft carriers. There had been a three-way split between those who retained an undiminished confidence in the ability of a properly handled battleship to withstand air attack, those who regarded battleships as obsolete and a waste of resources and those who tried to balance the conflicting claims of the more partisan advocates of artillery and air power. The conventional wisdom of the day was that the battleship remained the arbiter of sea power and queen of the oceans. The gun was generally regarded as the prime weapon at sea and aircraft were subordinate to it. The role of aircraft was seen to be the provision of reconnaissance beyond the range of cruisers, defense of the battle line and the securing of air supremacy over the battle fleet, to spot for guns and to carry out attacks on the enemy battle line, particularly when it was out of the range of the guns or in flight. In this latter role aircraft attacks were seen as essential if the enemy line was to be engaged and destroyed in an artillery duel.

The experience of the first two years of war was inconclusive in that the results of combat could be interpreted in various ways. Only one capital ship – the *Hood* – was sunk in a straight artillery duel, but the example of the striking power of aircraft as shown at Taranto could be discounted by a world holding small regard for Italian martial prowess. Neither of the extremes could draw much comfort from battle experience. The battle of Cape Matapan in March 1941, however, showed that an enemy in flight could be brought to a gunnery engagement after crippling strikes by aircraft, and the end of the *Bismarck* in May 1941 seemed to confirm this. The *Bismarck* was destroyed by artillery and torpedoes after she had been crippled by attacks by carrier aircraft. The lesson that had it not been for the successful air strikes the *Bismarck* would have eluded the forces hunting her and made the safety of a friendly port was widely realized, but what was little appreciated at the time was the

Left: The destroyers *Cassin* and *Downes* were wrecked in Drydock No 1.
Right: A floating crane salvages an Aichi D3A for analysis and evaluation by technical intelligence experts.
Below: USS *Shaw* rests on the bottom alongside the quay.

real lesson of the *Bismarck* chase. That was that the German battleship would have been caught and destroyed far more quickly and at far less cost had she been sought and engaged by strong, numerous and properly constituted carrier forces.

The Japanese attack at Pearl Harbor removed all these arguments within the United States Navy. Carrier aircraft had shown that at minimal cost to themselves they could destroy battleships far beyond the horizon range. As the Americans had no battle line left after the attack, they had to rebuild their tactical formations around the carriers. The war-winning Fast Carrier Task Group concept emerged directly from the Pearl Harbor disaster. The Americans had experimented with the idea in the inter-war period, but their exercises had proved inconclusive. Now, after Pearl Harbor, they had to make a virtue of necessity. Irreverently, the loss of the battle line at Pearl Harbor was almost welcomed in some quarters of the United States Navy. There were those who felt that what had been lost was only a collection of obsolescent scrap metal, of minimal fighting value. This was an overstatement, but it had more than an element of truth in it. Battleships still had a

major role to play, as time was to show, but they were now clearly subordinate to carrier aviation.

The concentration of losses among the battleships gave a distinctly misleading impression, because it served to disguise the simple fact that the overwhelming part of the US Pacific Fleet emerged unscathed from its ordeal. For the moment the Fleet had had its fangs drawn and was in disorder, but the major part of the US Pacific Fleet was intact and capable of action. The carriers, of course, were unscathed. The United States Navy possessed 18 heavy cruisers, 12 of them with the Pacific Fleet, but only three had been in Pearl Harbor at the time of the attack and none were damaged. Three light cruisers had been damaged, but these were only three of 18 such cruisers in the American fleets and their temporary loss did not lead to the withdrawal of any of the eight light cruisers in the Atlantic. Destroyers were in extremely short supply, but with 171 in service the loss of three could be absorbed. Not one of the submarines was damaged. With 112 already in service and another 65 on order, American submarine strength could only bode ill for a nation such as Japan so desperately dependent on sea communications for her very existence.

Left: The scarred bows of the battleship *Pennsylvania* in drydock during salvage operations.
Below left: A salvaged Val dive bomber is brought ashore.
Below: Only the superstructure and gun turrets of USS *Arizona* remained above water after her ordeal.

The attack on Pearl Harbor, therefore, can be seen as being at best no more than a moderately successful operation. Had the carriers as well as the battleships been caught and destroyed then the Japanese position would have been much stronger. The American position would have been correspondingly weaker than was the case, but in reality there was no means by which the Japanese could have destroyed or rendered ineffective the major part of the Pacific Fleet even by a series of strikes on the warships themselves. Yet this action was only the start of the war, and two consequences arose from this operation. Firstly, the strategic situation was such that, given Japanese resources, there was no point in the Pacific where the Japanese could reasonably hope to force the Americans to give battle under conditions favorable to Japan. There was no place that the Japanese could attack with reasonable hope of success and force the Americans to give battle against their will. Secondly, with the strategic initiative in the western and central Pacific denied them, the Americans for the moment could only react with tactical offensive action. This involved limited and peripheral carrier operations, snapping at the edges of Japanese main force undertakings, the commitment of the cruisers to action, and, most important of all, the unleashing of the submarines in an all-out unrestricted campaign against Japanese merchant shipping. The latter was to be critical in deciding the outcome of the Pacific war. Too much attention is focused on the great carrier battles. What ground the Imperial Navy down to defeat was the combination of the five great battles decided by naval aviation, a whole host of savagely fought actions – normally at night – between light forces and the unrelenting attrition of Japanese merchant shipping at the hands of American submariners. The submarine campaign was necessarily slow

to get into its stride, but in the end it accounted for more than half of Japan's total merchant shipping losses and brought the island empire to the brink of starvation. The submarines also accounted for many warships, including six of Nagumo's force. In 1941 the adoption of the submarine campaign by the Americans was a reflex action, forced upon the Americans by events, but it had devastating consequences for Japan.

There was, moreover, another aspect to the American campaign against Japanese shipping. What went largely unnoticed at the time was the hidden loss caused to Japan by her going to war. In 1941 Japan needed 10,000,000 tons of oceanic merchant shipping to sustain herself; she had only 6,000,000 tons under her own flag. The ships of other nations, mainly those nations with whom Japan went to war, made up the deficit. Thus, when she went to war, Japan lost 4,000,000 tons of shipping other than what she was able to capture or salve. In the event Japan was able to capture about 1,250,000 tons – at a time when her needs rose drastically. Among the losses at Pearl Harbor, therefore, must be counted some 2,750,000 tons of merchant shipping lost to Japan. It was an extremely high price to pay for eight battleships and 10 other warships and auxiliaries sunk or damaged.

The loss of this merchant shipping was catastrophic for Japan, but before the outbreak of the war the Imperial Navy never showed any awareness of the overwhelming importance of merchant shipping resources to Japan. The need for convoys and the general defense of merchantmen was neglected by a navy obsessed with the notion of battle with a numerically superior enemy. It was this obsession that blinded the Japanese to the critically important nature of the necessary back-up for a fleet – its fleet base complete with power stations, workshops, dockyards and oil dumps. Had the Japanese really sought to immobilize the Pacific Fleet by the most effective and simplest manner possible, they would have been well advised to have considered attacks not on the warships but on the dockyard facilities at Pearl Harbor. Without such facilities a fleet cannot operate, but the Japanese left them untouched. In 1940 and 1941 the United States Navy, working on a shoestring, had built up a reserve of 4,500,000 barrels of oil on Oahu. Most of it was stored above ground and was wide open to destruction from the air. Had the oil dumps and the other essential dockyard facilities – such as the power sources – been systematically attacked and destroyed, the Pacific Fleet would have been hard pressed to maintain even a minimal defensive stance in the central Pacific. The miraculous American recovery at Midway would have been impossible, and it is difficult to see how the Americans would have been able to make any strategically significant move for at least 18 months. The cost of rebuilding such resources – had they been de-

Left: A water-filled bomb crater on the apron at Hickam Field awaits attention, while repair work is started on the hangars.
Bottom: All that remains of this B-17 is the forward fuselage and the wings.
Below: President Roosevelt three months before Japan's surprise attack.

stroyed – might well have proved prohibitive in time and effort, but somehow given the vastness of American production, it is difficult to envisage how the ultimate outcome of the war could have been significantly affected.

Yet the material aspects of the Pearl Harbor operation pale into insignificance when set against the moral consequences of the attack. The Japanese believed that in attacking and destroying the Pacific Fleet they would leave the Americans frightened, confused and divided. They believed that the division between isolationists and interventionists in the United States was deep and a permanent feature of American political life. They could point to the fact that in the summer of 1941 the House of Representatives had come within two votes of abolishing the draft, thus doing away with the major part of American fighting strength. The forces of isolationism were indeed very strong in the United States but they were not so strong as to want peace at any price and they were not so strong that they could withstand the storm of righteous indignation that greeted the Japanese onslaught. Indeed, isolationist sentiment dissolved overnight as people who had been President Roosevelt's most bitter critics immediately pledged their loyalty and support to the Commander in Chief in the wake of the attack. The immediate reaction to the attack was not recrimination – though that was to follow – but to pledge all to total victory.

The Japanese plan of campaign envisaged a limited war. The Japanese idea was to fight a defensive war behind a firm defensive perimeter until the Americans, tiring of conflict and losses, would come to terms in a compromise peace. Pearl Harbor removed the very faint possibility that this might happen. If, as the Japanese believed, will is the most important element in war, then the war was already lost to Japan. After Pearl Harbor there was no possibility that the Americans would accept anything other than total victory or total defeat. The Japanese believed that their superior resolve would see them through against the odds, but when the President addressed the Congress on 8 December and asked for a declaration of war on Japan, he was speaking for a united roused democracy that could never be placated by half measures, that would not be satisfied with anything other than the total destruction of the enemy. As the President grasped the rostrum and denounced Japan, the lines of Longfellow – significantly from *The Building of The Ship* – which Churchill never tired of writing to Roosevelt, can hardly ever have seemed more appropriate:

Thou, too, sail on, O Ship of State!
Sail on, O Union, strong and great!
Humanity with all its fears
With all its hopes for future years
Is hanging breathless on thy fate!

Pearl Harbor was a victory for the Imperial Navy, but it was by such victories that Japan moved down the path of total defeat. Admiral Chuichi Hara commented after the war that Roosevelt should have pinned medals on the Japanese for the attack; nothing that the Japanese could have done could have proved more self-defeating. More than ships and men were lost that December Sunday at Pearl Harbor; what really perished was Japan's dreams of power and conquest. The tragedy was that it was to take 45 months to bring Japan to realize it – and it was only by a path through Hiroshima and Nagasaki.

6. EPILOGUE

Below left: Admiral Husband E Kimmel was C in C of the US fleet during the Pearl Harbor attack. He was held responsible for the poor defense of the base and dismissed on 17 December.
Below right: American sailors recover the body of a Japanese airman.
Below: America's recovery from the Pearl Harbor debacle was complete. Three cruisers are shown moored there in 1943.

Fortune was to reserve very different fates for the ships and indviduals involved in the Pearl Harbor operation. The US Pacific Fleet's Commander in Chief, Admiral Husband E Kimmel, was never given the chance to show his worth in war. He was removed from his command within two weeks of the attack and was replaced by Nimitz. Kimmel tried in the aftermath of the attack to retrieve something from the shattered ruins of his fleet and career by using his three fleet carriers to support the Wake garrison after it had repulsed a Japanese invasion attempt on 10 December. He was dismissed in the middle of the operation and Wake fell on 23 December with no attempt being made by the Pacific Fleet to prevent its loss. Kimmel, in effect, was made the scapegoat for the American disaster and was never employed again. The only comment that can be made upon his personal tragedy is to note that he was appointed to his command, the most prestigious command in the entire US Navy, over the heads of 32 more senior admirals, a recognition of talents he was never allowed to show in battle.

On the Japanese side personal fortunes were mixed. Fuchida and Genda both survived the war to become widely respected members of society in the new Japan. Fuchida became a protestant minister; Genda a Major General and Chief of Staff of the Japanese Air Self-Defense Force. Yamamoto was assassinated in April 1943 when a carefully planned American ambush caught his aircraft when he was on a tour of inspection of the upper Solomons. Yamamoto's aircraft was shot down in 1943. Nagumo, too, failed to survive the war. After the Midway disaster he was given command of the 1st Carrier Division – the *Shokaku* and *Zuikaku* – during the battles in the Solomons. After these battles had been lost he never again held a seagoing command and he ended his career and life as commander of Japanese forces on Saipan. He committed suicide when his forces were overrun.

The fate of the ships involved in the operations reflected the general outcome of the war. Only two of the battleships sunk at Pearl Harbor, the *Arizona* and *Oklahoma*, were destined to become total losses. The *Arizona*, along with the *Utah* which was also a total loss, still lies at Pearl Harbor. The *Oklahoma* was raised in 1944 in order to clear Battleship Row, but she was not taken in hand by the dockyards. By that stage of the war the US Navy had more than enough battleships to justify trying to recommission a ship 30 years old. She was sold for scrap, but sank while being towed to the West Coast.

The other three battleships that were lost, the *California, Nevada* and *West Virginia*, were all raised and entered the dockyards for reequipping and modernization. They emerged from the yards considerably better and more powerful than they had been before the attack. All three ships took part in operations off Iwo Jima and Okinawa. The *California* and *West Virginia* saw service at Leyte Gulf in the

company of the *Maryland, Pennsylvania* and *Tennessee*. The *Nevada* missed Leyte because of her service off Normandy and southern France. Thus all the battleships recovered at Pearl Harbor took their revenge in the final cornering of the Imperial Navy.

Of the carriers that were absent from Pearl Harbor two, the *Enterprise* and *Saratoga*, showed an instinct for survival that enabled them to survive much damage. Both saw the end of the war. The *Enterprise*, in winning 19 stars, gained more battle honors than any warship in American history. The *Lexington*, ferrying aircraft to Midway at the time of the attack, was lost to aircraft from the *Shokaku* and *Zuikaku* at the Battle of the Coral Sea in May 1942. The *Hornet* and *Yorktown*, in the Atlantic in December 1941, also succumbed in 1942, the *Yorktown* at Midway and the *Hornet* at the Battle of Santa Cruz in the Solomons in October. The *Hornet* was significant. Her career lasted a few days over a year. Within a year of her being sunk a new *Hornet* had been completed under the terms of the Two-Ocean Naval Expansion Act the Pearl Harbor operation had been designed to frustrate.

With the exceptions of the *Cassin* and *Downes* every other ship sunk or damaged at Pearl Harbor was brought back into commission. This included the *Shaw* and even the *Oglala*. The old minelayer showed powers of resistance to the salvage teams that she did not reveal on 7 December. She needed not one but two major operations to free her from the mud and get her afloat, and then she chose to sink again not once but twice. She then suffered a fire before she reached dry dock. Though the Americans might well have despaired of her at that stage, she was reconditioned and converted to serve out the rest of her time as a repair ship and PT-Boat tender. She was discarded in March 1947 when a venerable 40 years old.

The warships of the Japanese carrier force experienced fates that would have confirmed the very worst fears of Yamamoto and Nagumo had they been alive to witness them. The Imperial ships fought hard to the bitter end, but they could not withstand the overwhelming weight of firepower that the Americans were ultimately able to bring to bear. Nagumo's haunting nightmare of the vulnerability of carrier flight decks to bombing was brought home in the catastrophic battle of Midway when the *Kaga* and *Soryu* sank on 4 June and the *Hiryu* and *Akagi* sank the following day. All four carriers were lost to aircraft from the American carriers absent from Pearl Harbor on 7 December. The *Shokaku* and *Zuikaku* missed Midway because of the damage they had sustained at the Coral Sea; their absence was probably the difference between defeat and victory at Midway. The *Shokaku* was lost to submarine attack in the preliminary stages of the battle of the Philippine Sea, the *Zuikaku* to carrier aircraft at the battle of Leyte.

Both the battleships involved in the operation, the *Hiei* and *Kirishima*, were lost at Guadalcanal. Both were gunned to destruction, the *Hiei* being given the *coup de grace* by aircraft from the *Enterprise*. Five of the destroyers, the *Akigumo, Arare, Asakaze, Tanikaze* and *Urakaze* were lost to submarines while the remainder, the *Hamakaze, Kagero, Kasumi* and *Shiranuhi* were lost to naval aircraft action, though the *Kagero* was first crippled by mines. Two of the destroyers, the *Hamakaze* and *Kasumi*, were lost during the last despairing sortie made by the Imperial Navy in defense of Okinawa. These destroyers shared the fate of the mighty 70,000-ton battleship *Yamato* which was overwhelmed by aircraft from nine of the carriers of Task Force 58.

What the *Yamato* could not survive mere cruisers could not hope to resist. The heavy cruiser *Chikuma* and the light cruiser *Abukuma* succumbed to air attack at Leyte Gulf, the heavy cruiser to naval aircraft, her lesser colleague to Army bombers. Thus in our list to date 19 of Nagumo's 20 ships have had their fate related, and 12 of them were destroyed either by air action alone or by air action in conjunction with another means of destruction. All but one

Left: American servicemen killed at Pearl Harbor are buried with full military honors.

of the 12 fell to carrier aircraft – a striking comment on the failure of Nagumo at least to search for the American carriers after the Pearl Harbor strike.

After the Okinawa action which saw the end of the Imperial Navy as a fighting force, just one of Nagumo's original ships remained, the heavy cruiser *Tone*. Perhaps her fate was the cruellest irony of all, coming as it did just three weeks before the end of hostilities. The last survivor of the ships that had steamed half way across the Pacific to strike the US Pacific Fleet in its lair was in turn sunk by aircraft from carriers while she rested at her moorings in the shallow waters of her base at Kure.

APPENDIX

Abbreviations

Standard American designations are given to all naval ships:

CV	Fleet Carrier
CVL	Light Fleet Carrier
BB	Battleship
CA	Heavy Cruiser
CL	Light Cruiser
DD	Destroyer
SS	Submarine

The use of an asterisk denotes a flagship.

Summary of Japanese Oiler, Submarine and Warship Losses by Year

	Oilers	Sub-marines	War-ships	Total
1941		1		1
1942		7	7	14
1943	3	10	1	14
1944	4	10	10	24
1945		1	3	4
Surrendered	1	1	1	3
	8	30	22	60

Summary of Japanese Surface Warship Losses by Location

The Battle of Midway	4
The Battle of the Philippine Sea	1
The Battle of Leyte Gulf	4
Okinawa	2
During the Solomons campaign[3]	3
In other theaters	7

Summary of Japanese Submarine and Warship Losses by Cause

	Japanese Losses of							
	CV	CVL	BB	CA	CL	DD	SS	Total
Sunk by aircraft[1]	3	2		2	1	4	2	14
Sunk by aircraft and mines						1		1
Sunk by aircraft and warships			1				3	4
Sunk by destroyers							11	11
Sunk by submarines	1					5	3	9
In surface engagements[2]			1				5	6
To unknown marine causes							5	5
Total	4	2	2	2	1	10	29	50
Surrendered at the end of the war						1	1	2
Grand total	4	2	2	2	1	11	30	52

[1] Carrier-based and land-based aircraft.
[2] Sunk by gunfire, ram and torpedo by any type of surface warship, including destroyers.
[3] Plus 10 submarines lost in the course of these operations.

Composition and Fate of Japanese Forces engaged in the Pearl Harbor Operation

1 Surface Warships and Auxiliaries

(a) The Pearl Harbor Strike Force: commander Vice-Admiral Nagumo.

(i) The Carrier Force. Vice-Admiral Nagumo.

1st Carrier Division				
CV	*Akagi**	Damaged by carrier aircraft, scuttled,	5 Jun 42	Midway
CV	*Kaga*	Sunk by carrier aircraft	4 Jun 42	Midway
2nd Carrier Division				
CVL	*Hiryu*	Damaged by carrier aircraft, scuttled	5 Jun 42	Midway
CVL	*Soryu*	Sunk by carrier aircraft	4 Jun 42	Midway
5th Carrier Division				
CV	*Shokaku*	Sunk by submarine attack	19 Jun 44	Philippine Sea
CV	*Zuikaku*	Sunk by carrier aircraft	25 Oct 44	Leyte Gulf

(ii) The Support Force: Vice-Admiral Mikawa

3rd Battle Division				
BB	*Hiei**	Sunk by gunfire and aircraft	13 Nov 42	Guadalcanal
BB	*Kirishima*	Sunk by gunfire	15 Nov 42	Guadalcanal
8th Cruiser Division				
CA	*Chikuma*	Damaged by carrier aircraft, scuttled	25 Oct 44	Leyte Gulf
CA	*Tone*	Sunk by carrier aircraft	24 Jul 45	Kure

(iii) The Screening Force: Rear Admiral Omori

1st Destroyer Flotilla				
CL	*Abukuma**	Sunk by land-based aircraft	26 Oct 44	Leyte Gulf
DD	*Akigumo*	Sunk by submarine attack	11 Apr 44	Philippines
DD	*Arare*	Sunk by submarine attack	5 Jul 42	Aleutians
DD	*Asakaze*	Sunk by submarine attack	23 Aug 44	Philippines
DD	*Hamakaze*	Sunk by carrier aircraft	7 Apr 45	Okinawa
DD	*Kagero*	Damaged by mines and sunk by aircraft	8 May 43	Solomons
DD	*Kasumi*	Damaged by carrier aircraft, scuttled	7 Apr 45	Okinawa
DD	*Shiranumi*	Sunk by carrier aircraft	27 Oct 44	Leyte Gulf
DD	*Tanikaze*	Sunk by submarine attack	9 Jun 44	Philippines
DD	*Urakaze*	Sunk by submarine attack	21 Nov 44	Formosa

(iv) The Supply Train

Kyokuto Maru	*Kenyo Maru*	*Kokuyo Maru*	*Kyokuyo Maru*
Shinkoku Maru	*Toho Maru*	*Toei Maru*	*Nippon Maru*

With the exception of the *Kyokuto Maru* all the ships in the Supply Train were lost.

(b) The Midway Assault Force: commander Captain Konishi

DD	*Sazanami*	Sunk by submarine attack	14 Jan 44	Yap
DD	*Ushio*	Surrendered		

Total Force: 22 warships and 8 oilers.

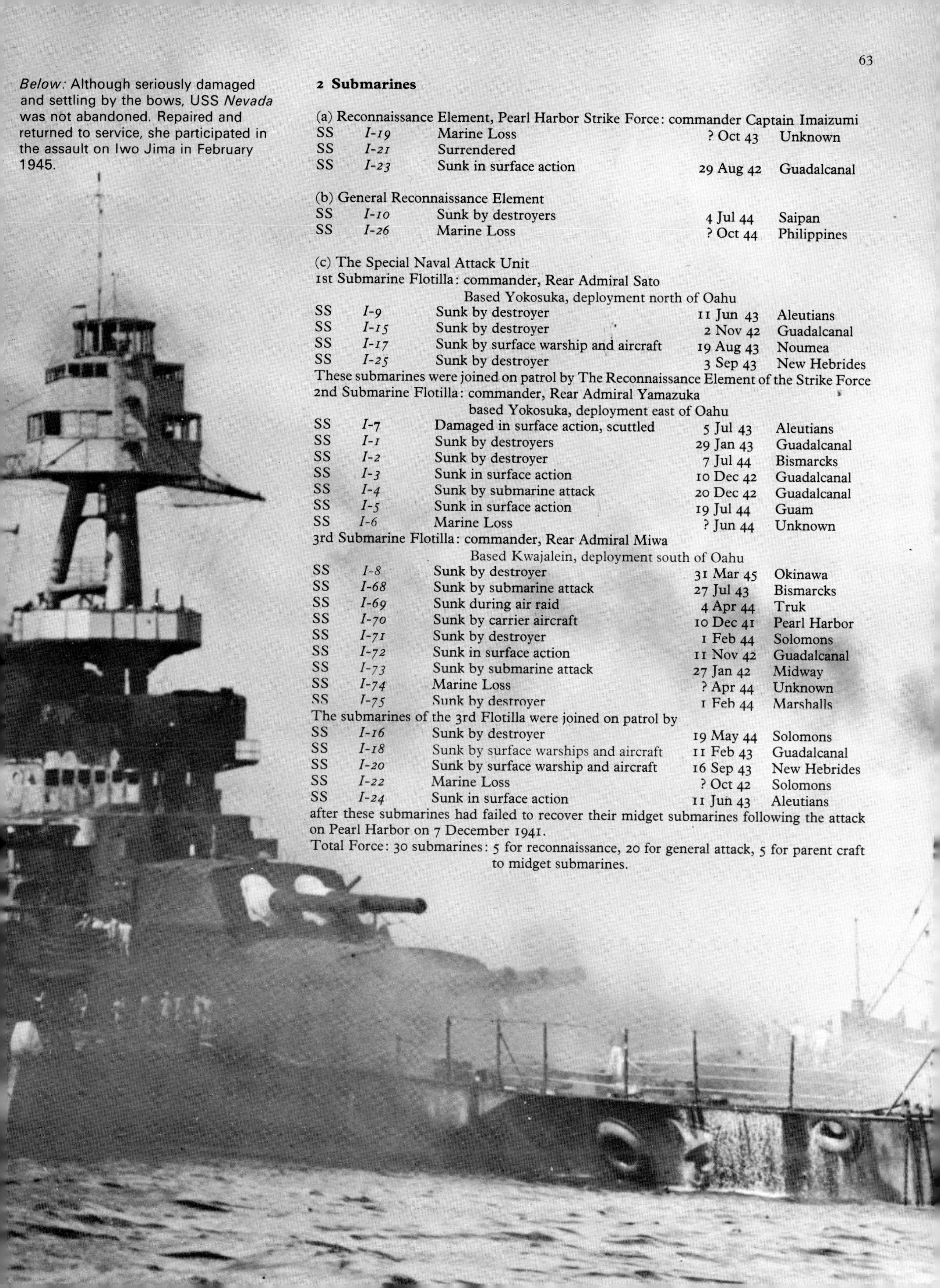

Below: Although seriously damaged and settling by the bows, USS *Nevada* was not abandoned. Repaired and returned to service, she participated in the assault on Iwo Jima in February 1945.

2 Submarines

(a) Reconnaissance Element, Pearl Harbor Strike Force: commander Captain Imaizumi

SS	*I-19*	Marine Loss	? Oct 43	Unknown
SS	*I-21*	Surrendered		
SS	*I-23*	Sunk in surface action	29 Aug 42	Guadalcanal

(b) General Reconnaissance Element

SS	*I-10*	Sunk by destroyers	4 Jul 44	Saipan
SS	*I-26*	Marine Loss	? Oct 44	Philippines

(c) The Special Naval Attack Unit

1st Submarine Flotilla: commander, Rear Admiral Sato

Based Yokosuka, deployment north of Oahu

SS	*I-9*	Sunk by destroyer	11 Jun 43	Aleutians
SS	*I-15*	Sunk by destroyer	2 Nov 42	Guadalcanal
SS	*I-17*	Sunk by surface warship and aircraft	19 Aug 43	Noumea
SS	*I-25*	Sunk by destroyer	3 Sep 43	New Hebrides

These submarines were joined on patrol by The Reconnaissance Element of the Strike Force

2nd Submarine Flotilla: commander, Rear Admiral Yamazuka

based Yokosuka, deployment east of Oahu

SS	*I-7*	Damaged in surface action, scuttled	5 Jul 43	Aleutians
SS	*I-1*	Sunk by destroyers	29 Jan 43	Guadalcanal
SS	*I-2*	Sunk by destroyer	7 Jul 44	Bismarcks
SS	*I-3*	Sunk in surface action	10 Dec 42	Guadalcanal
SS	*I-4*	Sunk by submarine attack	20 Dec 42	Guadalcanal
SS	*I-5*	Sunk in surface action	19 Jul 44	Guam
SS	*I-6*	Marine Loss	? Jun 44	Unknown

3rd Submarine Flotilla: commander, Rear Admiral Miwa

Based Kwajalein, deployment south of Oahu

SS	*I-8*	Sunk by destroyer	31 Mar 45	Okinawa
SS	*I-68*	Sunk by submarine attack	27 Jul 43	Bismarcks
SS	*I-69*	Sunk during air raid	4 Apr 44	Truk
SS	*I-70*	Sunk by carrier aircraft	10 Dec 41	Pearl Harbor
SS	*I-71*	Sunk by destroyer	1 Feb 44	Solomons
SS	*I-72*	Sunk in surface action	11 Nov 42	Guadalcanal
SS	*I-73*	Sunk by submarine attack	27 Jan 42	Midway
SS	*I-74*	Marine Loss	? Apr 44	Unknown
SS	*I-75*	Sunk by destroyer	1 Feb 44	Marshalls

The submarines of the 3rd Flotilla were joined on patrol by

SS	*I-16*	Sunk by destroyer	19 May 44	Solomons
SS	*I-18*	Sunk by surface warships and aircraft	11 Feb 43	Guadalcanal
SS	*I-20*	Sunk by surface warship and aircraft	16 Sep 43	New Hebrides
SS	*I-22*	Marine Loss	? Oct 42	Solomons
SS	*I-24*	Sunk in surface action	11 Jun 43	Aleutians

after these submarines had failed to recover their midget submarines following the attack on Pearl Harbor on 7 December 1941.

Total Force: 30 submarines: 5 for reconnaissance, 20 for general attack, 5 for parent craft to midget submarines.

INDEX

Acknowledgments

The author would like to thank
Jane Laslett, the editor
Adrian Hodgkins, the designer
Penny Murphy for preparing the index
Richard Natkiel for supplying the maps
Tony Robinson for writing the captions
Jinbo Terushi for supplying the artwork on page 19

Picture Credits

The author would also like to thank the individuals and agencies listed below for supplying the pictures:
Bison Picture Library: pp 10 (both), 11, 22 (left), 25 (top), 26, 28 (bottom), 48, 58 (top)
Robert Hunt: pp 27 (top)
Imperial War Museum: pp 1, 17 (top)
Manchini Newspapers: pp 7 (all three), 57 (top)
Masami Tokoi: pp 14 (both), 20 (center and right), 21 (all three)
National Archives: pp 1–3, 4–5, 28 (top), 32 (both), 33 (bottom), 34–35 (both), 38–39 (both), 40–41 (all four), 42–43 (all three), 44–45 (all three), 46 (both), 47 (top), 49, 50, 52–53 (all three), 54–55 (all three), 56 (both), 60 (main pic), 61, 62
Shizuo Fukui: p 13 (top)
US Air Force: pp 24 (top), 29 (top), 30–31 (all three), 57 (bottom)
US Army: pp 29 (below), 33 (top)
US Navy: pp 9 (all three), 12 (both), 13 (bottom), 16, 17 (bottom), 18 (top), 22–23 (both), 24–25 (bottom), 36 (all three), 47 (bottom)